west marin review

Catherine,
with love & gratitude,
[illegible]

2015

06

A Publishing Collaboration

POINT REYES BOOKS • NEIGHBORS & FRIENDS

VOLUME VI • 2015

PROSE

POETRY

ART + ARTIFACT

MUSIC

Paola Martin, Grade 6, *Canada Goose,* paint and pencil, 8½ × 11 inches

LESLIE
ALLEN

Dear Reader

WELCOME BACK to the *West Marin Review*. Marcia Balian's Jack-In-The-Box cover inclines us to warn you to stand back and be ready for a surprise, but if you're a returning reader you know to expect the very best poetry and prose here, and a gallery of extraordinary art. This is the sixth volume featuring new works, produced by a small band of volunteer designers and editors and Point Reyes Books. Many of our contributors come from this rural place, tucked into the folds of the Point Reyes National Seashore and the Golden Gate National Recreation Area, influenced by history here and what nature serves up daily. But you wouldn't call the *Review* a "history" or a "nature" magazine. Its content is as broad and as inclusive as your imagination. In these pages, we do look back in time, we do explore the natural world, but we also dream and ponder, and tell true stories and make some up.

Nor are our contributors confined to West Marin. The artists, poets, writers of fact and of fantasy in this volume come from across the United States as well as from around the corner. They are from nine years old into their nineties, they are brand-new writers and artists, and writers and artists many times published.

Though the *Review* doesn't publish to a particular "theme," as many journals do, national and even world events sometimes spin a collective thread that may be seen in art, in poetry, in the mood if not the content of a story. That has happened in this volume in the recollections of Robert Kroninger in "Japs Not Wanted in Winters" and of David Miller in "I Be Loving My Neighbor's Wife," and in Elisabeth Ptak's "Charles Dickens and Ferguson."

Leslie Allen, *Clear Spring Trough Above the Pacific, Valley Ford,* 2014, oil on linen, 24 × 18 inches

Other surprises register high on an emotional scale. Read "The Rancher Whispered" by Denise Parsons, and Frances Lefkowitz's "Two Very Short Stories" and see if you don't agree. Observe Roy Mash swoon in his "La-Z-Boy" recliner. And then, for something completely different, take a 25-mile ride in Susan Starbird's mind on her way to work in "Commuting Through the Valley of Death."

A splendid portfolio of marine algae as animate as ribbon dancers, as delicate as crochet lace, is excerpted here from Peter Connors's collection. There are other startling, almost other-worldly images: T. C. Moore's lumbering "Hay Nets," Ashley Eva Brock's mysterious "Shoe Creature." And you'll discover poetry that evokes image, too, as in Heather Altfeld's "Indian, Wild (Ishi)," with its simple, haunting opening: "On the last night of the long confinement,/as he walked beneath the bright moon" and Sabine Sabec's rollicking "The Origin of a Piano": "A bang of the left hand/got the right hand singing."

On that musical note, you are invited to follow us 'round the mulberry bush, to crank up the volume, support the *Review* as a reader, and join our family of contributors. Submission guidelines are at our website: westmarinreview.org.

POEM Tobi Earnheart-Gold, "Spring"
ART Elizabeth Sher, detail from *Arbres arrencats d'ametles (Uprooted Almond Trees)*, 2010, archival pigment print on rag paper

Spring

Even the potatoes
Sprouting in the cellar's dark
Seem to know

Light

Larry Ruth

Choose green, not sea green, not yellow green.
A dark forested shade. Bamboo and the willows
remind me of the late afternoon, light running
through tall grass and water at Kern Kaweah
Canyon, granite and reflection, sound and silence.

All day I sat, reading *Light,** a day in the life
of Claude Monet, from his first cigarette, rolled
before daybreak, tiptoeing past his wife's bed
at half past four, on his way to an appointment
with lilies, water, and dawn.

I read for hours, following Monet,
spending a day in the mountains, my day
remade as I read of Monet's lunch with family
and friends, scarcely bothering to eat my own,
absorbing the mood at Giverny, and the food,
from soup to *ragoût* to *salade*. Glasses of wine.
On to dessert. A meal lasting from noon to dusk.

At four I thought of you, of his lilies painted
in pages of this book, those we saw at Musée Marmottan,
how we lingered in the gallery before eating
our own lunch down the street, the sun
moving overhead, hours slipping past
sharing *salade, saumon, bière à la pression,*
conversation and laughter.

I forget now if I'm writing about reading,
reading about writing, or remembering
the warm afternoon and how we
ate and drank and talked before
finally noticing the changing light
and that it was late
and beginning the walk home
to your flat on Cité du Cardinal-Lemoine,
where the name on the button read 'Brown'
and the light in the foyer
didn't work, and in late afternoon
a few rays of sunlight filtered
down the well behind the stair.

---

*Eva Figes, *Light,* New York: Pantheon, 1983.

Mary Siedman, (opposite) *Highway One Trees,*
(above) *Magnolia,* both 2014, oil on canvas, 40 × 30 inches

Two Very Short Stories

Frances Lefkowitz

MOONWALKING

BONES ARE white, not beige, and they get whiter the longer they are exposed to the elements. They become lighter in weight as well as color, as attackers both minute and mammalian find them delicious, circle and swarm and pounce. We pick them up at the beach, my children and I, on a January day that should be gray and wet and cold, but instead is clear and dry and warm. One son has an aversion to dirt, wants to make it disappear from his body as soon as it appears. He would never use his hands to lift something found on the sidewalk. But in the sand by the saltwater, all is clean. We drag the bones, and sticks as bleached and smoothed as bones, tracing maps of where we make our footfalls. We miss our long hibernation; we are desperate to bundle and close down away from weather. But the rain won't come, and the sun won't stop burning the clouds, bluing the sky, forcing us outside.

The sea anemones are fleshy and pink, they look like slugs and also like those parts of the human anatomy that I am grateful I don't have to discuss with my children quite yet. My girl and her dirt-averse younger brother say, "Eww" when I place my finger onto the sticky tentacles to show how they curl up, fist-like, at intrusion. The older boy says nothing, but neither does he give it a try.

They line up in a row behind me, quiet and slow as astronauts, as we venture onto the ledge, pockmarked with water-smoothed holes, so it really does seem like we're walking on the moon. I feel their vague fear, or at least awe, at the frothing waves in the near distance crashing against the rock, rattling our own bones. So I still have a chance to mother them, and they can still sibling each other, and on this dangerously warm day I am overcome with my own awe, which is suddenly outweighing my fear.

Right now, I am not listening to anyone spreading theories about when we're going to lose our food and our water, our oil and our air. I am not worrying about the drought and the water table. I am walking on the shore with my children, over the rocks, then back onto the sand. I am spreading a blanket and they are flopping down on it. I am falling in love with the three of them sharing the covers and reading their books as I watch over them.

Eva Bell, age 12, *Calla Lily,* 2014, tempera , 11 × 8½ inches

THE BACKWARD QUADRUPLE

MY HUSBAND is moping, as if maimed. He's just dropped off our daughter at gymnastics practice.

"What's the matter? Did something happen?" I ask. I'm on the couch, my hand shielding my eyes from the hall light.

"Nothing," he says, dropping his coat on the chair by the doorway.

But something is festering, I can tell by the canopy of norm he's working so hard to conjure. Haven't I mothered enough today, I think, but I don't say it. Instead, I wiggle my pinky, try to get him to at least feign a laugh, then open my arms and invite him in. He hesitates. The look blazed across his face: is that guilt?

"Come on," I say, and he drops to his knees but doesn't lean into me.

"They asked me to leave," he says. His voice is shush and his eyes are focusing on the lightning-bolt scratch in the plaster of the wall that we haven't yet filled.

"Why?" I say. My voice is steady. I mean, I'm a social worker in a city hospital, what haven't I heard?

"I guess I was looking too hard." He describes the girls, in leotards, their bones and flesh on display, their hair pinned up to show every jutting. These girls are not yet teenagers, though a few have the roots of curves starting to emerge. To watch them as a group is to see larvae in each stage, to see creatures whole and yet also in the act of becoming something else. "It's like I could see Jessie as she is now, and how she was six months ago, and then what's going to happen to her in a year," he says, mortified by the inevitable. "I tried to focus on the mat, the backward quadruple whatevers."

He's crying now, and though his willingness to tear is one of the reasons I fell in love with him, I do not always carry a hanky. For my husband now, I am strong and dapper; I comfort and amuse, brush away doubts. Then I get him to start dinner while I pick up Jessie, and by the time I walk out the door he's rinsing spinach and singing along to the radio.

It's steamy inside the gym, and lithe bodies are bending and folding and leaping and hanging and falling and bouncing and rolling and furling and unfurling. The beauty of these girls is indeed astonishing, and it lies not in their perfection, but in their mere unbrokenness. What man or woman could be prepared for the sight of bodies so unconsciously becoming themselves, the clock ticking under the skin, the hormones hiding, ready to pounce and protrude and break skin and ruin everything? I am reminded of foals, prancing from sheer instinct and a green meadow and a mother standing by.

Jessie spots me, comes running, and she's still young enough to open her arms and grab my waist, let me kiss the top of her head. But it's the sight of her feet that makes me gasp. How could I not have noticed their size, so large for her petite frame. She lets go of me to get her bag from the locker room, and the creature I see loping away has bones extending up and out, a ghost of her future self. I can't stop staring, wonder if I will be asked to leave.

The Olives of Olive Drive

Scott Mossman

The olives of Olive Drive
Fell for boys with sneaker treads to squish.

We ran and played and felt
Like we were happy

With radio cars and soft serve
Every other weekend.

He tried so hard.
We tried so hard

To crush the insides out,
To stain the sidewalk purple.

Natalie Chavarria (top left), Izabella Guiterrez (top right and bottom left), Viviana Villalobos Gonzalez (bottom right), all Grade 4, *Sunflowers,* 2014, watercolor, 14 × 9 inches

The Sespe

Sabine Hoskinson

BEYOND OJAI and my rich but rugged boarding school, up Horn Canyon and over the ridge, the Sespe Wilderness—for me always hot and dry, all sage and spiky, flowered yucca—becomes a backyard. It's part of Southern California's Los Padres National Forest, and Sespe Creek is still a wild river indifferent to dams and concrete channels.

I horse camped with school horses in the Sespe when I was fifteen. It was fall and the trails were dusty as the horses hoofed across switchbacks and through dry meadows. We were seven riders and two packhorses. We were teenagers. Our faculty leader, a plain-spoken horseman we called Ox, knew everything and brought along two junior wranglers-in-training. They were seventeen and, in the way that I did then, I chose one to silently love. His name was Pete. Pete spoke rarely, but when he did his words were quick and cocky.

Once, we swam our horses into a wide pool of the river. We rode them bareback into the water and slipped off their backs, backwards over their buttocks, as they began to swim. We trailed behind them, towed by fistfuls of their tails. Other times we swam and the girls sunbathed on rocks in our underwear—we pulled in our stomachs and pushed out our chests. At night we hiked by foot up skinny trails, narrow like deer paths, to smelly hot springs in turquoise plastic tubs.

When we rode in the afternoon heat, the sweet smell of sage and the sun's warmth seeping through my jeans made me sleepy. In that sun, or at night when I pulled the sleeping bag over my head, breathing the faded fruity smell of sunblock and bug spray, I thought of how Pete's tanned hands once tightened my drooping saddlebag straps, leaning from his horse to mine. He never really said my name, but I imagined it.

On the last day, we rode out before sunrise. Our climb over the ridge into Ojai was long and steep, and we started ahead of the smothering heat. The trail wasn't maintained and the overgrown path caught us in dim moonlight. With the trail lit by our headlamps and swaying glow sticks tied to our saddle skirts, Ox picked a slow path and we followed. We gave the reins full slack and let the horses bend their necks low to see the trail—their night eyes better than ours.

Ahead in the line, a horse stepped off of the dirt trail and struck his hoof against a rock. The horseshoe scraped and sparked against the stone. "No!" the rider yelped as she pulled her horse to the canyon side of the trail.

I was a rider but this was something else. My legs clenched around my horse's sides and I talked to myself. Shit, I don't like this.

Halfway through the climb, we rested on a plateau.

"Everyone dismount and check your girths," Ox said as he stepped off his horse and readjusted a packhorse's panniers. "Tighten them if you need to and give your horse a pat."

My fingers trembled as I pulled at the leather latigo.

"If you hold my horse, I can help." Pete gestured his reins towards me and I moved aside. "Are you scared?" he asked, looking at me over his shoulder as he wedged three fingers between the rope girth and the horse. "It looks fine," he said and he pulled the stirrup back into place. My hands still trembled.

"Are you scared?" he asked again.

"No," I answered.

"Okay, high five," he whispered and held a hand up in front of me. I gave it a gentle smack and blushed in the dark.

I rode behind Pete until we reached the sunrise and the ridge. I rode behind Pete down Horn Canyon, past the third, second, and first water crossings, until the school's pastures were in sight.

Back at school, Pete wore Wranglers and cowboy boots to class with the tightly curved bill of a school cap shading his face. In the afternoons, I'd see him trot his horse past the dorms out to the gymkhana field with one finger through a belt loop or his spare hand tapping time against his thigh to his horse's step. At dinner, his hair was flattened and dull without his cap on; he looked smaller than before in his crumpled school coat and tie.

"Hey," he'd say sometimes, but it wasn't ever the same.

La-Z-Boy

Roy Mash

for Anne

The footrest swoops up out of nowhere,
and you are rocked back, launched

into indolence, carried off and tenderly set
before the momentous affairs in the TV.

Better than any womb, better even
than your cousin Larry's chiropractor,

this posture: somewhere between rescue
and abduction, every muscle exactly where

it wants to be, and you yourself at the helm
of your life, imperious, snoozing.

Red Rocker

Jon Langdon

WE HAD several hot days last May, temperatures in the low 90s, unusual for this time of year on the California coast in the small town where I live. On one of those days, I was sitting, as I usually do after lunch and a brief nap, in a red rocking chair on the covered front porch of the local feed store, which is pretty much located in the exact center of our three-block business area. From the vantage point of the red rocker on the shady porch several steps up from street level, I could look down and out on our main street for some distance in either direction, seeing foremost the town's largest restaurant on my immediate left and the post office (housed in the old railway depot) on my immediate right, and across the street the historic old saloon, the barber shop, and the large garage, as well as other shops and businesses up and down the street.

As I sat in the stillness and heat and gazed out on the street, it struck me that the normal noonday hustle and bustle of people and vehicles was totally absent, except for two lone cars parked kitty-corner across the street. Not a soul to be seen, and the silence was eerie and complete. Looking past the large, opened doors of the garage into the dark cavern that it was, I made out the figure of Hilary, the garage manager, in the doorway of her small office about fifteen feet in from the sidewalk. She was unmoving and appeared to be languishing against the door jamb, looking out from the garage's dark interior toward the whitewashing light outside. It was then that I realized I was looking at an Edward Hopper painting: the sharp contrast of light and dark, of interior and exterior, the solitary figure looking off in profile, the absolute quietness of it all, and the sense that time was standing still.

While thinking of Hopper and his work, I also felt I was in the middle of some deserted midsummer prairie town, empty because all the farmers and their sons were out in the fields harvesting the summer wheat. Back at the farmhouse the wives and daughters were cooking the midday and evening meals to be delivered to the men, saving them the round-trip trek between farmhouse and the distant fields where they worked. The younger children, after their chores, were swimming and fishing in the local creeks under the shade of embankment willows.

Tipped back in the red rocker, I wondered where these vivid images of the prairie came from. Driving trips through the Plains states in an RV with my ex-wife, Mary, many years past; Willa Cather books read so long ago; Steinbeck's *Grapes of Wrath;* old movies? I remembered jerky, grainy, black-and-white newsreels of bare-chested men with long forks lifting great loads of wheat high up into the open hoppers of threshing machines.

More likely, today's farmers are young ag school grads riding up high in their air-conditioned, fully automated, GPS-directed harvester while listening to the wraparound sound of Garth Brooks and Kenny Chesney.

It's not always like this sitting for an hour on the feed store porch. Once I wrote a poem, and sometimes I've been known to tip my fedora and take a quick nap. But usually it's a coffee and a crossword that occupy my time or a visit with a tourist whose wife is shopping inside the feed store's gift shop, or a local who will stop for a chat. There are two red rockers on the porch, and although I'm often alone, feel free to come by. I enjoy a good visit and consider it time well spent. To paraphrase Robert Frost, I could do worse than sit on the feed store porch and rock the Red Rocker.

Indian, Wild (Ishi)

Heather Altfeld

On the last night of the long concealment,
as he walked beneath the bright moon
four sleeps down from the mountain
toward the prickle of lantern-light in the valley,
did he still stop to dust away his footprints,

to sprinkle dried leaves over his steps,
did he crawl on his belly through the runway
of rabbits and weasels rather than walk the wide berth
of bears, did he allow one small twig to surrender and break
in the pitchy blackness, listening to its split dry sound?

The creek he left behind in the darkness
vowed to keep turning and tumbling in his absence.
The boulders vowed to rest beneath the stars.
The stars vowed to remain seated in their dark nests.
The trees screened any shadow that might lean

into their trunks. The wisps of smoke from each tiny fire
he had made against the rocks remained in the wind.
Dragonflies rose in the blue afternoon
when he arrived at the jailhouse,
bent and worn, asking for nothing,

or asking, maybe, for something—
the pitch of one voice calling to another,
that clattering of sound, a whole echo
rising out from a throat, up into
the uncertain particles of light.

Eytan Schillinger-Hyman, age 16, *Serengeti Solitude*, 2014, oil and pen on canvas, 16 × 20 inches

Pacific Marine Algae

Pressed Specimens by Peter Connors

BODEGA HEAD, CALIFORNIA

SPECIES: *CALLOPHYLLIS PINNATA*
LOCATION: HORSESHOE COVE DATE: 19 AUGUST 2004

I HAVE BEEN studying the distribution of the more than 160 species of macroalgae along the Sonoma Coast. Our local algae grow in habitats ranging from sheltered sand and mudflats to the most wave-swept outer coast rocks, and many species only grow attached to other species. In extreme cases, a single alga attached to rocks may have four or five other species growing on it. This lifestyle, called epiphytic, is possible for marine algae because unlike terrestrial, vascular plants, algae do not have roots, and they absorb necessary nutrients directly from seawater through all their tissues.

My pressed scientific specimens are a way of showing the beauty and diversity of marine life along the northern California coast. Documenting marine algae is also valuable to students and researchers as climate change, development, and worldwide pollution induce changes in our environment.

SPECIES: *ULVA LINZA* LOCATION: CAMPBELL COVE SANDFLATS DATE: 7 AUGUST 2005

Ulva linza grows on intertidal rocks and sand flats along the Sonoma Coast in areas protected from heavy surf. Its bright green color and slender, ruffled ribbons make it the loveliest of the green algae, Chlorophyta.

SPECIES: *ULVA CLATHRATA* LOCATION: CAMPBELL COVE SANDFLATS DATE: 17 SEPTEMBER 2005

The thin, hair-like tendrils of *Ulva clathrata* bear little resemblance to the rest of the *Ulva* (sea lettuce) genus. This small, bright-green alga grows in protected bays and estuaries, either attached to rocks or free-floating as a dense mass.

SPECIES: *CALLOPHYLLIS FLABELLULATA* LOCATION: DRIFT, DORAN BEACH DATE: 12 AUGUST 2000

The beautiful alga *Callophyllis flabellulata* grows on subtidal rocks or on other algae in the Bodega Head area. It is classified as a red alga, Rhodophyta, named for the characteristic pigments that give most species in this group a reddish tint.

SPECIES: *MICROCLADIA COULTERI* LOCATION: DRIFT, BODEGA HEAD NEAR JETTY DATE: 26 JULY 2005

Microcladia coulteri is a common epiphytic alga that grows on other algae in the Bodega Head area. It is classified as a red alga, Rhodophyta, named for the characteristic pigments that give most species in this group a reddish tint.

SPECIES: *DESMARESTIA HERBACEA* LOCATION: SOUTH JETTY, BODEGA HEAD DATE: 16 MAY 2014

Desmarestia herbacea grows on low intertidal and subtidal rocks along the Sonoma Coast. It is classified as a brown alga, Phaeophyta, named for the characteristic pigments that give most species in this group a brown color in life, often tinged greenish when dried.

Farallon Stories

Jennifer Kulbeck

IT IS early evening and the sun has yet to set. Light is falling out of the sky and the wind is up and steady from the northwest. Water is washing into Little Murre Cave in the Shubrick Point area of South Farallon Island, thirty miles west and slightly south of San Francisco. It is April and the surface water temperature is the lowest of the year. A large boulder near the mouth of the cave breaks the force of the surf so that water pours in under and around it.

The cave opens to the east. When the sun is low in the sky at the end of the day, the rocks and ledges above the cave cast long shadows over the east side of the rock and onto the water.

The island is made of granite and quartz. The floor near the back of the cave is sand. It is dark in the shadow of the cave and the lower walls are covered in sponges and anemone. Bat stars wrap around cobbles and stretch flat on the walls. Some are red, some are orange and purple, some are mottled brown. The webbing between their arms is a heavy blanket and a wet sail. They are attached to land. They will not be lifted by the northwesterly wind or carried away with the current.

April is almost laying season, and above the cave the Common Murres are croaking and growling and turning their chins to the sky for attention. The rock is crowded with nesting pairs. They are puddles of white against black and rock. They have black feathers on their heads and backs and wings and their underbellies are white. Their bodies are better for water than for wind. Small, heavy wings make take-off difficult. Murres are more maneuverable under water and can dive to depths of 100 to 200 feet. They have thin, pointed bills and small round tails. Their faces are white in winter, with dark spurs behind the eyes. They are oily, feathered torpedoes.

From inside the cave, as the sun sets, the shadow of a murre laying an egg stretches across the ocean surface. Moving with the waves but dark and still, it is a phoenix: body lifted upright, wings half outstretched. The egg emerges after five or ten minutes. Giant green anemones stretch their tentacles wide and contract again. Bat stars grip the rock. A group of seabirds fly together in a line, just above the surface of the water. And the sun sets.

The egg rests on the open ledge. A murre, undisturbed, will sit on an egg for thirty days before it hatches, to keep it warm and guard against gulls and other egg thieves. The egg is large and pointed at one end. When it is jostled and nudged it rolls in a circle rather than falling off the ledge. Each egg, white, grey, blue, brown, has its own pattern of freckles in black or lilac. The chick is born downy, with dark feathers on top and white below. The nesting pair takes turns diving for fish. They carry one at a time, lengthwise, with the fish's tail hanging out the end of their beak. Leaning forward against the rock, making a tent with its wings, the murre curls its neck, forehead down, and as the fish slides out the side of the beak, the chick swallows the fish head first.

Seabirds cover the jagged rock. Still unable to fly at three weeks old, chicks hurl themselves off the ledge and hit the water. They dive. They chase fish—small schooling forage fish and polar cod and capelin. They learn to use their wings to propel forward underwater. They dive deeper. They eat sand lances and sand eels, sprats, cod, and herring. They find mollusks and crustaceans, marine worms and squid.

The wind direction shifts. Later in the fall, when the northwest winds decrease and the surface water warms, the water will hold a clear blue color and the zoo-plankton will return. In the winter, when they are not nesting, the murres will rest on the water and call to each other with a soft purring noise. The sun will set many times. Little Murre Cave will fill and empty. And spring will return.

In the busy days that followed the Gold Rush of 1849, clipper ships and other vessels sailed into San Francisco Bay in large numbers. There was no lighthouse. Ships relied on maps and moons and captains' guts to navigate the approach. A clipper called the *Golden City,* which sailed from New York, reported she was stalled in fog for five days off the Farallon Islands. Others sailed blind into the jagged shelf.

Many men came through the city for pickaxes and pans, brothels and hot baths, horseshoes and work boots, titles to land, and extra hands. Food. Biscuits, cakes, omelets, and brown bread. Soup, meat, and coffee. Folks hadn't yet planted much farmland or thought to keep chickens. Eggs were in short supply.

The Common Murre lays eggs with a fiery red yolk and a tough shell. Each egg is two or three times the size of a chicken egg. Nesting grounds for a dozen species of seabird and shorebird, the Farallon Islands are home to the largest Common Murre colony in the United States outside of Alaska and Hawaii. In the mid-1800s, the seabird eggs were selling for a nice profit in the San Francisco food markets. A dozen of these eggs, which are said to taste like chicken eggs, could fetch more than a dollar.

Egg-picking entrepreneurs traversed the Farallons all year, and especially in the laying season from May to July, chasing the birds off their nests and making their claim. Individual eggers established their territory. They would first move through and smash every egg they could find, then the next day and each subsequent day they could be certain every egg they collected was fresh. Murre eggs did not keep long. Eggers had to work quickly to shoo the birds and pick the eggs before the gulls could move in and snatch them. The hard shells helped prevent too many cracks, but with their swift steps and the crumbling rock under their feet, many men slipped down into the surf or, worse, fell forward onto their bulging vests, the oozy waste a bright, expensive mess.

Egg on their face. Fiery red yolks. Regrets. Missteps. Broke.

Thomas Wood, *Northern Point Reyes Peninsula & Bodega Head,* 2014, oil on canvas, 24 × 30 inches

Meanwhile, back in Baltimore, Maryland, on a bright and significant afternoon, Francis X. Kelly called down the hall to Francis A. Gibbons. The hall was dark and the sunlight came in on a white angle and cut through the dim. The Treasury Department had awarded their construction firm the contract to build lighthouses in California. Men and supplies soon set sail on the *Oriole* to San Francisco. It was 1852.

When they first arrived on South Farallon Island they met with an unexpected setback. Egg-pickers with bent backs, standing shoulder to rounded shoulder, prevented the construction crew from coming ashore. When the crew returned with a U.S. Coast Survey ship and a landing party of armed soldiers, the egg-pickers surrendered the shore.

Stone for the construction of the lighthouse was quarried on the island, and the masonry of the tower was lined with brick. Workmen carried the material up the sharp slopes. The bricks for the tower went up in bundles of four and five on the men's backs. It was slow going across the uneven rock, always against the wind.

The egg-pickers and the lighthouse construction crew kept an eye on each other as they went about their work. Together, they battled the wind and the weather, with chapped red faces and determination. They knew each other's stories of overnight fog and the ghosts of moons, of loneliness, of the breaking waves that tore through their boats and tangled their oars, of the endless seasickness, of blood in the water, of the great white sharks that plucked baby sea lions from the edges of the shore. They knew them all.

The Farallon Island Light first shined on October 15, 1856 from the highest peak of the Southeast Farallon. Shipwrecks continued, by folly and fog, but were fewer, even as more clippers made their way into the San Francisco Bay. The construction crews moved on and the lighthouse keepers came ashore. The new men suffered the weather, the water, the great whites, the isolation, and the egg-pickers all over again.

Some keepers moonlighted as egg-pickers to supplement their government wage. Claims on seabird colonies were overlapping and tension built. Competition for the eggs was fierce. Pickers carried protection and camped out among the seabirds to hold their claims.

At its height, the egg trade pulled in more than 500,000 eggs a month. Egg companies organized, and the individual eggers and the lighthouse keepers persisted. The stakes were high. An armed group of eggers tried to force the keepers off the island. Keeper Amos Clift wrote to his brother: "We are now in the midst of the egg season, and the egg company and the light keepers are at war." It was the Egg War of 1863. The tension had turned to conflict. Two men died.

The keepers continued egging and the demand for eggs held. Keeper Clift was soon removed from the Lighthouse Service for trying to monopolize "the valuable privilege of collecting eggs." In 1881 the federal government took sole possession of the islands and made egging illegal.

The construction firm of Francis X. Kelly and Francis A. Gibbons built eight lighthouses in California. They were the first lights of the West Coast.

Charles Hoehn, *West Bay,* 1934, photograph provided by the artist's grandson, Paul Sevcsik

Because There Is Loss

Erin Rodoni

We keep driving until the light
fires the wasteland red,

until tarmac

towns shadow to sky,
palms signing

oasis. How quick
the places we have been

leave us. The beloved shines
between date fronds,

saddles camelback,
lifts the lip
of its tent. We crack

the motel's coffined gospels,

unpack

noun after noun—*rib, wine,*
bread—The beloved lies

just ahead.

After Wendell Berry's Window Poems

Jody Farrell

How fine
to have a
many-windowed house
that looks
to a mountain.

How fine
to have an old tree
where a buzzard
airs his out-spread wings.

How fine
to have a morning
with nothing in it
but a mountain,
a tree,
and an empty space
where the buzzard was.

Leslie Allen, *Spaletta Ranch Barns, Valley Ford,*
2014, oil on linen, 28 × 22 inches

Stunts

Michael Taylor

WE SPENT the afternoon running power cables and placing lights all around the Bronson Caves, a dry, dusty canyon carved deep into the hills of Griffith Park. It was late summer of 1981, four years after I'd come to Hollywood, and I'd taken a call to day-play as a juicer on a low-budget feature film called *The Sword and the Sorcerer.* They'd be shooting a big night-exterior scene, and night work always means lots of lights and cable. At the time, I was still making the transition from the grind of low-budget feature films to the world of television commercials, where the pay was better and the work considerably less time-consuming. But I wasn't quite there yet, and day-playing, or working for a day on features, allowed me to work with old friends and occasionally make some new ones, all while earning a paycheck.

This promised to be a long night—"movies 'til dawn," as the saying goes—but the beauty of day-playing is that it's always a temporary gig, and you can put up with almost anything if it's just for a day.

Besides, making movies was still fun back then.

As the sun dropped below the canyon rim, we took a break from laying cable to watch the filming of a stunt designed to simulate a man being thrown off a cliff to his death—a murder that would spark one of the central dramatic conflicts in the story. Stunts have long been an integral part of the cinematic experience, and in many ways represent the distilled essence of movie-making: using skill and artifice to create a convincing illusion. Watching a well-executed stunt is an education, the experience drawn into sharp focus by the element of danger and an undeniable frisson of excitement. Early on, one of the fun things about working on feature films was the chance to see a wide variety of stunts performed right before my eyes. It was like going to the circus as a kid to see the high-wire and trapeze artists toy with gravity under the Big Top, only now I was part of the circus.

Stunt men aren't wide-eyed fools nursing a death wish, but professionals who want to do their job and drive home in one piece at the end of the day, just like everybody else. Although their livelihood often depends on skating along the thin edge of disaster, they work hard to minimize risks. Every aspect of a stunt is meticulously planned and rehearsed until the actual performance becomes almost automatic. Very little is left to chance—but if the element of risk can be minimized by such thorough preparation, it can't be eliminated altogether. Proper execution of the stunt is crucial. When the cameras finally roll, the stuntman and his team must do everything *exactly* right to avoid serious injury, or worse.

I found a spot on the canyon floor with a clear view. High on the cliff above the caves stood a man dressed in a medieval costume, playing a character about to be thrown to his cinematic death by the henchmen of an evil tyrant. The stuntman stood there, staring down at his target 65 feet below, a fully inflated airbag surrounded by boulders. He stared for a very long time. The crew waited, cameras ready, watching that lonely figure up there on the cliff. A nervous quiet settled in over the set. The tension mounted. At last, the stuntman signaled a thumbs-up and stepped back from the edge, out of sight. The Assistant Director called for the cameras to roll, and once all were up to speed, he nodded at the director. "Action!" the director yelled. Nothing happened for a long moment, the tense silence broken only by the mechanical whir of film rolling through cameras.

I stared upward, forgetting to breathe, then watched that man run right off the cliff into thin air.

I'd seen high falls before, the stuntman diving, arms extended to either side, feet slightly apart, in a graceful arc designed to plant him flat on his back in the center of the airbag. When properly executed, such a stunt ends with a loud *whump!* as the airbag absorbs and dissipates the enormous amount of energy the stuntman's body picked up during the fall. He then leaps off the bag with a huge, adrenaline-fueled grin, shaking hands with everyone around. It's quite a sight when everything goes right. But if something goes wrong—if he should land head or feet first, or off to one side of the bag—that's trouble.

This fall looked all wrong. Instead of a smooth dive, the stuntman came off the cliff at an odd angle, his head down, arms and legs dog-paddling furiously. The thought flashed through my mind how realistic this seemed, as though it really was a man falling to his death rather than a carefully planned illusion. A heartbeat later, he hit with a sound I'll never forget—a muted, crunching thump as his legs hit the airbag while his entire upper body smashed onto the boulders.

A paralytic silence gripped the set until one of the special-effects crew broke the spell and ran to the crumpled body to attempt mouth-to-mouth resuscitation. It was a futile gesture. Later, he told me the stunt man's head, cradled in his hands, felt like "a bag full of broken glass."

I'd just watched a man throw himself into eternity.

Someone laid a blanket over the body while the rest of us milled around, unsure what to do. Three women sat together and cried as the men stood stiff-legged and silent, each of us trying to process what had happened. An ambulance finally arrived. Two paramedics loaded the body inside, then drove away.

Twilight had slipped into darkness by the time the Line Producer emerged from his motor home to call a wrap. We were done filming at Bronson Caves, he said, and wouldn't be coming back.

There was nothing left to do but begin the grim task of wrapping the heavy equipment and carrying it back to the trucks. One of the young grips, a kid barely into his twenties, tripped and dropped an armload of gear. Close to tears, he unleashed a gushing torrent of profanity. Eventually, we got the trucks loaded. Only the grips, juicers, and two drivers were left. A case of beer appeared. Somebody passed a hat, taking up a collection for the wife and baby of the dead stuntman. His name, I learned, was Jack Tyree. We sat there in the darkness amid the glow of cigarettes, drinking beer and talking into the night.

I wish I could report that some sort of epiphany came out of this to make sense of it all, to put Jack Tyree's death in perspective. Like everybody else on the crew, he'd gotten up that morning and gone to work to earn a paycheck—in his case, $1,200, or so I heard. That was pretty good money back in 1981, but hardly worth dying for. While the rest of us drove home to bed and a restless night, Jack Tyree was already there, in the words of Raymond Chandler, sleeping "the big sleep."

My phone rang much too early the next morning. It was the Best Boy, asking me to come back to work on *The Sword and the Sorcerer* for one more day, filming on a soundstage that served as the production company's home base for the duration of the shoot. This was the very last thing I wanted to do, but turning down work is a cardinal sin in the freelance world, where one dares not risk angering the fickle gods of Hollywood. Besides, the crew needed help, and in a way, I was still looking for some kind of closure on that awful night before. I drove to the stage a couple of miles west of downtown Los Angeles, then worked with the lighting crew until we broke for lunch. As we headed back on stage afterwards, the Best Boy called me into his "office"—a tiny desk with a chair inside the lighting truck.

"We need a couple of guys to go back and rig lights inside the cave," he said.

"The same lights we wrapped last night?"

"Yep."

"The producer said we weren't going back."

"Yep," he repeated, with a weary shrug.

And so I found myself back at Bronson Canyon, hanging and powering lights inside the cave at a location the producer had solemnly promised, not twenty-four hours before, we'd never see again. This wasn't the epiphany I'd been seeking, much less closure, but rather a crude, that's-the-way-it-is affirmation of the oldest cliché in Hollywood: the show must go on.

Movies are highly contrived dramas designed to hook and hold our interest for a couple of hours. People sit down in a movie theater expecting to see a seamless execution—a story featuring interesting characters who face and overcome situations more starkly dramatic than anything most of us ever encounter in real life. A good movie is an entertainment, casting a spell that allows us to forget our own problems for a little while. In those movies, characters often suffer horrible, graphic deaths, but no matter how convincing, the audience knows deep down that it's make-believe. Other than the occasional bent and bloodthirsty sociopath lurking in the dark, nobody goes to a movie hoping to see actual injury or death up there on the screen, but it happens in the movie industry more often than most civilians realize. The outside world rarely hears about these accidents unless a well-known actor is involved, but film industry workers are killed and injured on the job every year. I've heard of dozens who have died on sets over the decades I've been in Hollywood. A camera operator and a stunt woman I worked with early in my career were later killed on other productions—he in a helicopter crash during the filming of a music video, she when what was supposed to be a simple fall from the roof of a two-story house went wrong. A grip I knew suffered a lingering death in the hospital after a heavy cart laden with equipment tumbled off the tailgate of a truck and nearly broke him in half. The industry throws a thick blanket over such accidents, keeping them out of the news with the rest of Hollywood's dirty little secrets.

The Sword and the Sorcerer was released in the spring of 1982 and went on to gross nearly forty million dollars—not bad for an independent film that cost only two million to make. The producers honored Jack Tyree in the credits, and I can only hope they steered some portion of their profits to his widow and child. Despite Hollywood's seedy reputation, there really are decent people throughout this industry who quietly go about their business doing good things—but I have no idea if the producers of *The Sword and the Sorcerer* are among them.

It has been more than thirty years since I watched Jack Tyree plunge to his death, and the image remains burned into my brain. We'll never know why that stunt went so wrong. Some of the veteran crew members told me they'd never seen a stunt man stare down at his airbag for such a long time before performing a high fall.

It's possible he over-thought what he was about to do and psyched himself out, or maybe his feet became tangled in that final instant before plunging into the void. All I know is that in the many thousands of days I've worked on set since that grim evening—on feature films, television shows, commercials, and music videos—I haven't had to see anybody else die, and for that I'm grateful. Although there have been many changes in my life and career since then, one thing remains the same: I don't like to watch stunts anymore.

In memory of Jack Tyree
September 12, 1943 – August 25, 1981

The Rancher Whispered

Denise Parsons

WHAT I remember most fondly is the Ramblin' Jack Elliott performance in the tiny diner. Well, not so much the performance itself, although it was quite special, but the fabulously stout middle-aged rancher who sat behind us. I'd seen him around town, always sporting a big bold belt buckle and fine felt cowboy hat. Toward the end of the night, as Ramblin' Jack described one of his last songs, *Old Shep,* about a favorite dog he'd taken on the road, the rancher whispered quietly to the woman beside him, "I love this song, but sometimes it makes me cry."

Linda Weyl, *Old Barn on "101,"* 2011, oil pastel, 14 × 20 inches

Close to the Earth

Jed Myers

We're the ones who must matter
to someone. I've planted the tulip
bulbs for winter, each hidden

under the mulch, its own bright idea
ready to press its slender agenda,
to open its red or its yellow

self-evidence, like an answer
to no one's or anyone's interest,
into the light when the sun's arc slips

over the shed. My wishes go
with the tulips, whose wishes do not
exist. Someone in spring might

blush, when I hand her the bunch
I'll cut close to the earth, blooms
that say nothing to themselves

or each other. We're the ones
who must each search for a mirror,
loosed by our births as we are.

Theodore D. Echeverria, *Poppies Celebrate the First Rains,* 2013, acrylic, 17 × 24 inches

Return to Sinkyone

Barbara Finkelstein

In memory of Graham

Had the rescuers known to leave him,
had the knowledge of deer prevailed,
he might have rested in the grass
as it moistened with fog that afternoon.
Had airlift not been by plane
but by dark birds circling, ones he said
he would someday gladly give his body,
becoming their eyes, their wings,
he could have died in this meadow,
this meeting of earth and sea and sky.

Had I carried the knowledge of deer
and been able to wait beside him,
close in the grass, my breath soft,
his breath slowing, quieting,
then there would have been no hands
on him, no metal pressing into him,
no sounds rushing through him
startling his injured brain.
There would have been sea wind,
sky wind, the dark birds calling.

Charles Eckart, *On the Mesa—Point Reyes*, 1992, etching, 3¼ × 5¼ inches

From *Old Hatch's Almanac*

Hal Ober

January 27, A Rooster's Step

Birds are good messengers. They're one of our most available liaisons from that club we sometimes forget or deny we belong to—nature. Sometimes the message they carry is simply, "This nuthatch is here." The surprise, delight, or other emotion that message elicits varies widely. A flock of pigeons wheeling over a town center, leaving one building for another, might be the epitome of the ordinary. But we'd probably miss them if we didn't have them, for mysterious reasons.

The other day it was milder than it's been here in Boston, in the thirties, and in the hardware store parking lot I heard a robin give its ordinary *cook-cook-cook!* exclamation from a nearby bare tree. The very normality of it meant something—that it wasn't as cold or as forbidding as it's been. It was a day more inviting of a casual remark.

Because of the cold and a Parkinsonian tendency to blame inertia on Parkinson's, my encounters with birds outdoors have been minimal lately. And there have been plenty of enticements. An article on the front page of *The Boston Globe* told about the appearance of snowy owls lately on local beaches, fields, at Logan Airport. The snowy owl is a messenger from the semi-mythical north: a spectral white gnome in the dunes who doesn't come down here very often.

Bob Kubik, *Good Morning*, 1998, block print, 9 × 6 inches

If you spend your time mostly inside, you rely on reports or photos from people who do go out, like the account I got last week from birder friend and jazz scribe Ed Hazell. On Martin Luther King Day, he went out to Plum Island and saw: "A bald eagle at Lot 1. A low flyover snowy that was so spectacular and so unexpected that I nearly drove into the marshes. A rough-legged hawk was hovering and hunting near the North Pool and I had a really long look. The sun was in and out of the clouds and when it came out, it lit up the hawk splendidly."

In addition to raptors, the bum saw horned larks (little masked marauders with tiny black devil horns, like someone's rude graffiti in a bird book come to life) and snow geese, and a northern shrike (bigger, big-headed masked marauder).

When you have a banner day like Ed's, it's enough to be able to fit these new acquaintances into the system of birds. Each one individually is "this bird here," but what do we know about the "here"? I don't mean the habitat, I mean the kind of bird Internet, the society of birds the messengers represent and report from, whether a ghostlike snowy owl or a drab gang of pigeons.

It's good to experience it directly, off-center and in rough context, but indirect communicates, too. I sometimes wonder how much of a birder Emily Dickinson was, to write "Hope is the thing with feathers." Hope is certainly what drives birders to go out, but Emily didn't get out much, they say. Nowadays, her friends would be emailing her nest-cam and YouTube links all the time.

Another friend, Hilary, commenting on my brief note some weeks ago about daylight lingering later, wrote: "I just read that every day gets a rooster's step longer."

I pause to let my readers run that movie of a rooster stepping across a barn floor, setting down its spraggle-toed, corncob feet with care and deliberation.

Hilary had read this almanac-worthy comparison in an issue of the *Seed Savers Exchange,* in an essay by co-founder Diane Ott Whealy, who passed along this observation from her grandmother. Whealy conceded that one rooster step may be paltry, but a few hundred rooster steps can bridge the distance between a cold winter's night and a warm summer evening. "You can get a lot done with a few more rooster steps."

This, too, is a bird message—a message from a bird who showed it and a person who got it, translated it, and passed it on. We could all benefit from such collaborations.

February 2, The Groundhog Variations

I had a lot of time to think about Groundhog Day today. I was stuck in the waiting room of Career Source, where an Unemployment Rep holds court every Tuesday and Friday. I was waiting to refile my claim. I was #31, sitting at a table with #29, a man with a trim beard and an organized manner. People sat around with books and crossword puzzles, looking solemn, bored, wary.

I wrote:

I'll be ready if someone comes out with a clipboard and asks us, "Does anyone know what day it is?" Some people will answer, "Tuesday" or "February 2nd." But when she calls on me, I'll say, "Groundhog Day." "That's right," she'll say, and others will wince that they missed the answer. It could cost them a job referral. "And what is the significance of Groundhog Day?" she'll go on.

This time someone else rushes to answer, but in his haste he gets it backwards. "If he sees his shadow, it's going to be nice. If he doesn't, it's going to snow?"

I raise my hand confidently. "If he sees his shadow, he'll get an interview. If he doesn't, it may mean he doesn't exist. And if he doesn't exist, his claim will be delayed. So that's why, to ensure that you cast a shadow, you should always carry a light source with you, like a flashlight or a candle. Hence the other name for the holiday: Candlemas."

She nods. "Which rhymes with?"

"Handlebars."

"Blunderbuss."

"Mandelbaum."

She marks something down in her clipboard that may have relevance to our future. Six more months of unemployment? A shovel-ready job destroying woodchuck habitat?

There follows a spelling bee that consists of one word: Punxsutawney. Only I get it right, and I add that it comes from the Delaware Indian word meaning "village of sandflies."

At this point, someone is shaking my shoulder. I lift my head from the table.

"Number 31," a lady says.

"I have been here four-and-a-half hours," I say, following her to her cubicle.

"I've been here eleven years," she replies. "What is your favorite holiday?"

"Groundhog Day," I answer carefully.

She writes that down. "Why do you consider the groundhog a role model in an uncertain economy?"

"You've got to take what you can get?" I guess.

She frowns slightly.

"Um. And whether he actually sees his shadow doesn't matter. It's that he got out of his burrow and *looked*." She smiles this time.

"If you could be any—"

"Groundhog."

"—animal besides a groundhog, what would you be?"

"Grog hound. No, ground squirrel. Aardvark."

"Take this seriously, please."

"How can I when your eyes are so bewitching?"

This time my shoulder is shaken more roughly. It's a tall, heavyset man with tattoos and a goatee. "We're closing," he says. They've turned out most of the lights.

"How long have I been asleep?" I ask.

"How the hell should I know?"

I pick up my stuff, shuffle to the door, then turn. "Just tell me one thing. Did I see my shadow?"

He grins, revealing metal teeth. "You're looking at him, pal."

Cue sinister laugh. Fade to February 3.

Jacqueline Mallegni, *Wabi-Sabi Basket,* 2013, rattan, waxed linen, paper-covered stone, and encaustic medium, 18 × 20 × 13 inches

¡Mi día en México!

Jocelyn Mata

I remember the smell
of fresh homemade *chilaquiles*
Hearing the *salsa picante*
sizzle in the pan
at my grandmother's house
en México

I remember the sound
of the door slamming *en la tarde*
Everybody racing *para comer chilaquiles*
at my grandmother's house
en México

I remember the taste
of cold *paletas de mango con chile*
Hearing the bells *del paletero* all day
at every corner *hay muchos niños en fila*
en la plaza, en México

With all these things *se te hace agua la boca*
el antonjo de comerte todo lo que está en cada esquina
Eating every day *en familia*
Y el sabor de Coca-Cola todos los días
¡I love *me familia asombrosa!*

Adah Pinchuk Hyman, *October Sunset, Tomales Bay,* 2011, oil on canvas, 24 × 20 inches

Vanessa Waring, *Everyone's Invited,* 2012, watercolor and gouache, 18 × 24 inches

I Be Loving My Neighbor's Wife

G. David Miller

I AGREED to meet with Jim McPhearson at the Old Ebbitt Grill for a late lunch. We hadn't been in touch for years, ever since I quit the government and moved to California. The Old Ebbitt was an odd choice, made perhaps more out of nostalgia for the old days than for its food or promise of a quiet conversation. One block from the White House, it had always been a bit louche—but now it was overrun by tourists in shorts taking up excessive space and decibels, and holding cell phones at arm's length, snapping that requisite selfie for someone somewhere.

Jim and I had worked together in Afghanistan in the mid-'70s herding an unruly pack of Peace Corps volunteers recruited and trained to teach English in remote villages in the Hindu Kush. Why anyone thought a large presence of young, eager Americans with a can-do spirit would win the hearts and minds of the recalcitrant tribes of Pashtuns, Tajiks, Hazaras, Uzbeks, Turkmen, and Balochs was a mystery then and now.

We moved to a table way in the back that was a bit quieter and began to reminisce about Afghanistan's peaceful decade when Kabul was a stop along the road for world travelers heading east toward India. After a dozen oysters and several cold drafts, the conversation came around to Sebastian Fielder, one of those rare Peace Corps volunteers who had studied Farsi and Russian in college. I remember him telling me that he chose to come to Afghanistan because of the "sumptuous buffet of languages." After going through

Michelle Chayes, *Mermaid*, 2014, mixed media, 23 × 16 inches training as an English teacher, Sebastian disappeared from my radar. He had been assigned to a small school in a remote village far from the reach of modern transport in a valley of the mountains of Paktia province.

After we ordered another round, Jim began his story about Sebastian.

"As you remember, the volunteers that concerned us most were the ones we heard from continually. They either had problems, complaints, or a need for stroking or approbation that consumed the time of our limited staff. There were always a few who couldn't hack it and had to go home. Conditions were pretty rough. Those we heard from the least we considered to be our best volunteers. Fielder was one we heard from the least.

"We knew he was okay because he received and cashed his monthly stipend at the local post office in Lazah, about a half-hour walk from his village. And, once in every six months, he received and completed the standard bureaucratic form that served our need to calculate the Peace Corps' contribution to American foreign policy goals. It was not until the late fall, when all volunteers were to show up at the annual retreat in Jalalabad, that we began to be concerned. He never came.

"A few days after the meeting, I took one of our four-wheel-drive vans to go check up on him. I had never been to his village before, and let me tell you, it was not easy to find. By early afternoon, on the road between Chamkani and Gardez, a light snow had begun to fall, turning the dirt road into a muddy, icy slush. I was lucky to make fifty kilometers per hour. And, of course, there were no road signs. It was nearing nightfall when I reached a *chaikhana* next to an old sign indicating that the intersection for Lazah was yet another forty-five kilometers. I felt it prudent to stop and spend the night there.

"Inside, steam from the giant samovar brought the temperature up to just about bearable with a coat on. I ordered some samosas and two pots of tea. As you remember, we used one pot to wash the tea cup. I then spread my sleeping bag on a charpoy and crashed into a deep sleep.

"In the morning, the sun was out and I continued on. I made it to Lazah in the middle of the day and, after getting directions, proceeded by foot to Sebastian's village. After a half hour, with one enquiry at the small store, I found where he lived. The modest one room with latrine and kitchen in the back was constructed of the usual mud-brick and mortar. It was enclosed within a larger compound that had a covered well in the courtyard shared by several households. The door was open, so I went inside and waited for him to come home.

"While I was waiting, a Pashtun, bearing the usual black beard and dressed in baggy *peron tambon* and the *pakol* hat, arrived outside the window. He was carrying his gun with the requisite bandolier of bullets strung across his chest. He pushed the window open and sternly said to me in clear English, 'Fuck you.' He then walked away. As you can imagine, I found that rather unnerving.

"However, my disquiet was somewhat relieved when, shortly after that incident, Sebastian cheerily popped in the door and gave me a welcoming hug.

"We stretched out next to a charcoal brazier amidst piles of hand-woven woolen cushions and carpets and began to talk. I felt I had to share the recent incident of the face in the window. Sebastian smiled broadly and told me that the frightening fellow in question was Baraat, his housekeeper. As it turned out, Sebastian had introduced the phrase 'fuck you' to the denizens of his village as a friendly American salutation. Sebastian's skill as an ambassador of American culture was borne out as we later strolled about the village exchanging this warm greeting with neighbors in a spirit of good cheer.

"As we talked, Baraat brought us tea, and to my relief, left without further pleasantries. It was then that I broached the subject of Sebastian's failure to attend the annual meeting. 'I was planning to be there,' he told me. 'In fact, I'd been putting aside a considerable sum each month from my postal draft for travel all around Afghanistan and neighboring countries—there's little need for me to spend much of it in this village. I kept it in the ceiling.' He pointed to the straw matting above. 'Last month, I reached up through the straw for my cache to take out enough for travel to Jalalabad. I discovered that rats had crawled in and chewed it all up to make a nest. So it goes for my travel plans.'

"Sebastian insisted I sleep at his house and attend his English class in the morning, and I readily agreed. Baraat brought in dinner, added wood to the stove, and left us without speaking.

"We talked into the evening. Sebastian spoke about being a part of and apart from the intense life of the village, with no privacy except in his room. I sensed his relief in having me to talk to. By midnight, I was curled up by the stove and lay there listening to the silence, which was broken frequently by the distant howl of wolves, or dogs.

"The next morning, as I entered the one-room, mud-brick schoolhouse, boys and girls stood up stiffly and remained standing until Sebastian signaled them to sit. He then put them through their paces for me. Frankly, I was not prepared for it. In all the years I have observed English taught as a foreign language, I never saw anything quite like this.

"The students had in their possession only one verb: *to be;* as in *I be, you be, he be, we be, they be.* So: *I be eating, I be sleeping,*

I be going. Past and future were handled by *I be eating yesterday* or *I be happy you be coming tomorrow.* I found this truly remarkable, since he managed to bring the communication skills of these students far beyond what I had seen in classes taught elsewhere over the same duration.

"Later, walking back to my van in Lazah, passing an occasional pedestrian who offered me a friendly, 'Fuck you,' I realized that Sebastian had infected the entire community with jive talk. Sebastianisms. Often I wondered if he had gone too far. Volunteers could easily step over the edge of what is appropriate in a highly traditional society.

"I didn't hear from him for another twelve months, except to receive his semi-annual report. Then one day I received a letter from him asking to extend his time of service beyond the usual two years. Although such a request was not entirely unusual, it did not occur often. I thought I should check in on him again.

"I started out early, hoping to make it in one day. I need not have been concerned—over the year, the Russians had paved many of the roads in Paktia province, turning the Gardez-Chamkani road into a highway. Outside tents along the way, Russian workers in uniform huddled over dung fires. I arrived in Lazah by mid-day and still found it necessary to walk the short distance to Sebastian's village.

"I found him at home but barely recognizable. He had sprouted a beard and was wearing *peron tambon* and the wool *pakol* hat. We hugged and he again seemed pleased to see me. We went inside and found Baraat preparing lunch. I awaited his putative greeting, but to my amazement received instead a slight smile with a nod. Sebastian and I talked, exchanging news. He said he was occasionally able to pick up the BBC on short wave, and that was his contact with the outside world. He told me that he and his neighbors spend a lot of time conjecturing about the Russian construction project underway in Lazah. Rumor had it that it was going to be a hospital, but no one really knew.

"We then sat without speaking at his small table and ate lunch. It was Sebastian who broke the silence. 'I sometimes feel here that I have come home after a long voyage.' He had an ironic smile that made me think that he, too, was surprised to hear this.

"I stopped eating to give him my full attention. It crossed my mind that he had not conversed with an English speaker since our last visit, except perhaps in the patois he had created in his classroom.

"'Here in my village I had not seen the face of a woman since I arrived. As soon as a girl in my classroom reaches puberty she disappears. A woman stays in her house or moves about in the market covered by a *burka*. I now am able to distinguish one woman from the next merely by the movement of her hands, the way she walks, or by her voice.'

"'Do you speak with them when you see them in the market?' I asked.

"'Oh, yes, especially the mothers of my students. They want to be sure their child is doing well, like any parent anywhere. In fact, they revere me—my students and their families have given me the name *Aurang*, Pashtun for "the wise one." But even with these brief conversations in public, we must be circumspect, because lingering too long in conversation can raise questions.' Again, that ironic smile. I didn't know why, but I felt that I had come at a crucial moment for Sebastian.

"'You want to know why I am staying on and why I failed to show up at the annual meeting again,' he said to me.

"'I just want to know you're all right. Can you imagine what a furor there would be in the States if harm had befallen you?' I tried to keep my words as light as possible.

"'Jim, the truth is that I have fallen madly in love. And not even for a day could I bear to be away from her.'

"This announcement took me completely by surprise, and I quickly looked around the room. 'No, she is not here. But she is present constantly. My landlord's house shares this courtyard. One day I was standing in the doorway and saw his wife without her *burka* stepping out of the side door of their quarters on her way to their latrine. She stopped for perhaps five seconds and we made eye contact. Then she turned and ran the few steps to the outhouse door. Jim, she was the most beautiful woman I had seen in more than two years, or perhaps ever in my life.'

"'My God, Sebastian,' I whispered. 'Be careful. The two of you could be stoned to death in the village square.'

"'We are passionately in love. But we have never been able to express our love in words, even if by chance we meet in the market.'

"'I don't understand. How can you be sure? Are you exchanging notes?' I was beginning to suspect his prolonged exile was making him delusional.

"He went on. 'Within an hour after that incident, a child appeared at my door with a covered plate of food and said it was from Gulalai.' Sebastian looked demurely down at the floor then continued. 'That is her name, Gulalai. It means "beautiful flower." Such a queer feeling of intense excitement came over me that I could not eat. I immediately went to work preparing something of my own for her. To send her plate back empty would have been an insult. Over these two years, with not much else to do, I've spent a lot of time learning from Baraat in the kitchen. The next day, I summoned one of the children playing in the courtyard and instructed her to return the original plate filled with my own dish—a fancy *qabili palau* of lamb and rice.

"'This ritual has gone on daily for months with only one day's exception. It was a day of hell for me. I learned later that one of her children was seriously ill and she took him to a clinic in Lazah. As you can now understand, it was impossible for me to break the spell and leave for the annual retreat.'"

Jim paused in his story, looking at his watch. I offered to order another round, eager to learn how this strange love affair played out. But he needed to catch a train and told me that, after all, there was no conclusion to his story.

"After that third-year extension," he said, "Sebastian was officially mustered out of the Peace Corps. He requested the money due to him for his return ticket to the States. But as far as I know, he never bought that ticket, nor did he leave his village."

Jim got up, put some cash on the table for his share of the tab, and said, "And I never heard afterward about an eccentric American brought to tribal justice for whatever law Sebastian might have been violating. As far as I know, he's still there. And I swear, every time I hear an interview on the news with a Taliban leader, I half expect to hear him say, 'I be killing you tomorrow.'"

Boredom

Tobi Earnheart-Gold

That wide threshold
Between inattention
& the luminous afternoon

Terry Murphy, *Cat Nap,* 2012, oil on panel, 16 × 20 inches

T. C. Moore, *Hay Nets,* 2012, installation, hay, straw, and cotton

July 31, A Meditation

Catlyn Fendler

It is so quiet I can hear, across the road,
the cows munching grass, imagine
I can hear the dry scrape
of the mother's tongue up her pale calf's side.
What else? The staccato of crickets, cicadas,
and the unmistakable cries
of birds I've never heard before.
They pause on the wire, then flit
from one maple or another, tormenting
the black kitty busy tormenting
a fat, red-legged insect hanging on.

It is time for nesting, for sleep that
in the country means no little death,
no putting out the lights by pulling on
the mind's black hood—No need
to charm fear into a manageable darkness.
Out here there is singing—
at three a.m., urgency in the silence,
in small systems an alertness
to the pull of already descending stars.

I've thought of death, dreamed of death,
imposed death on every scene
until life and death have lost their meaning.
I see only these cattle,
glowing gold and sienna in the late, July light,
the catalpa throbbing its deep lime, still
in the slide of the gray, early evening.

Judy Levit, *Unanswered Questions,* 2013, acrylic and collage on canvas, 12 × 12 × 1½ inches

Flying

Chris Reding

THERE IS something captivating about the First Nations hoop dancer who is arching up on her toes and tapping flat on her heels to the rhythm of the chanting and drumming. The young dancer spins and twirls with her feet continuing to stomp to the drumbeat while she dances back and forth and moves a hoop up her arm. But it isn't her weaving a series of hoops into a perfect interlocking ball before collapsing them again that draws us.

This is the story of that eleven-year-old Lil'wat dancer who is also a cowgirl who races her pony to win in the barrel races. Today she is so filled with life that even her braids and the feathers at the tips shimmer to the rhythm of her dancing body. Singing out her pleasure and pride, her feet flash in and out of the hoops that she is weaving around her torso. Once, when she taps a hoop on the ground with the perfect pressure to flip it up into her waiting hand and it fails to move, she just looks at the audience and giggles. Then without losing a beat, she snaps her toe against the edge of the hoop again sending it up to where her arm could move smoothly through its center. Toward the end of her dance she begins spinning to the drum beat faster and faster, her feet moving to the quick rhythm as she works the hoops up her arms and behind her back until they link and become wings. Her face, enchanted, turns to the sky.

Her body arches poised to fly.

Anne Faught, *Journal Entry,* 2010, oil on canvas, 18 × 24 inches

Franz Kafka Dreams of Yosemite

Gary Thorp

> The Sarcophagid fly has evolved ears on its thorax to help it find singing cicadas. It crawls under the cicada's wings and lays an egg in the sound-producing organ. In response, the cicada may sing a "protest song" but this seems to have little effect.
>
> –John Muir Laws, *The Laws Field Guide to the Sierra Nevada*

When one is encroached upon,
one must sing
no matter what the result.

The voice may falter, squeak,
or fail us. Still, we must address
the Sarcophagid fly.

Ignore everything beneath your heart,
but pay simple attention
to what lifts you.

To the evolving ears of the world,
a song of protest, whatever else
it is, is still a song.

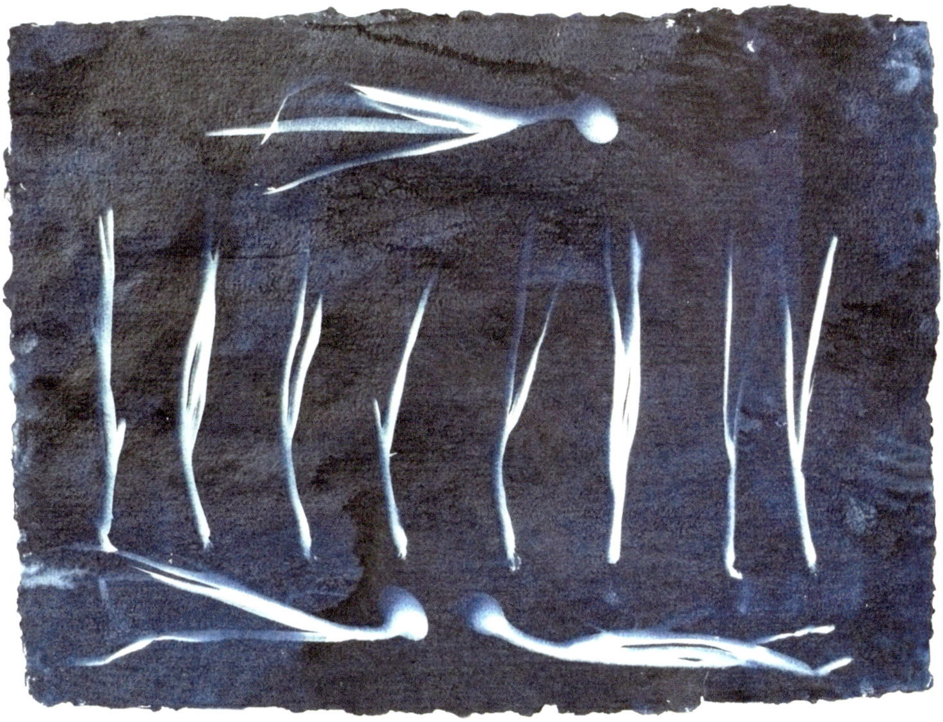

Mary K. Shisler, (top) *Turnips, and "Don't Think the Garden Loses Its Ecstasy in Winter"—Rumi,* 2014, tea-toned cyanotype on handmade Indian watercolor paper, 22 × 30 inches; (bottom) *Onions, Showing the Way to the Afterlife,* 2014, cyanotype on handmade Indian watercolor paper, 22 × 30 inches

The Complexity of the Sparrow

Betty Davidson

THE MORNING sun shines glorious above our kingdom. The sweet whistle of the songbird is life in its good nature. To ignore the pithy comments of individuals who appreciate the beauty and grace of such a special day is difficult but easy as well. For the world is like a cube of sugar. Small, sweet, one of many others. But it is our world. The only one we have known and the only one we have shared, though shadows may guide some as the sun to others. The light and the dark are two paths. And it is up to you and you alone to decide which life to abide by. The choice may be hard and may be simple. You must trust and live by the decision. But there is one thing we all know: the light and dark are not compatible and they will not prosper knowing the other is still there. How should I know? Because I am a princess.

Elizabeth Sher, *Arbres arrencats d'ametles (Uprooted Almond Trees),* 2010, archival pigment print on rag paper

Phenology

Lucas Benjamin

yesterday the crab apple by the house
today the lilac by the garden
I calculate star geometry
and anticipate the dogwood

me, I'm looking for the perfect stone
in the dark of rain at noon
and to measure my fortunes
by the roughness of my hands

Ward Walkup III, *summer, fall, winter...SPRING!* 2014, oil on panel, 8 × 10 inches

Japs Not Wanted in Winters

Robert Kroninger

I WAS a student at UC Berkeley in the 1940s, driving home most weekends to work on the family farm in Yolo County's Capay Valley, on a route taking me through Winters and other small farm towns along the way. I changed the route abruptly one day toward the end of World War II.

In early 1942, soon after the United States entered into World War II, all people of Japanese descent in the western U.S. were compelled to go into internment camps far from the Pacific coast. One of the farm families in the Capay Valley was Japanese, the children classmates of my brother Dick and me. On the day they had to leave,

Mother, Dad, Dick, and I went to their farm and helped pack the limited belongings allowed at the internment camp. They had to leave most of their lifetime of belongings, as well as their lovingly tended farm. We shed tears with them, embraced, waved them good-bye and wished them a speedy return. Caucasians eagerly took over their fertile farm, as was done on Japanese farms all over California.

Now, three years later, toward the end of the war, as I approached Winters in my Ford coupe on my drive in from Berkeley one weekend, I saw a sign nailed to a utility pole, reading in large print, "WE DON'T WANT ANYMORE JAPS IN WINTERS."

With the war drawing to an end, Caucasians who had benefited from the ouster of the Japanese by taking over their farms now feared they might have to give them up to the returning owners. I stopped and tore down the sign, took it with me to the farm, and burned it. On my way back to Berkeley, I saw that an identical sign had been posted at the other end of Winters. So I tore that one down, too, and trashed it when I got back to the fraternity. Two weeks later, identical replacement signs were up again, and I again tore down the one south of town on my way to the farm. On my way back to the university on Sunday I stopped to tear down the replacement sign at the north end of Winters. As I was getting out of my car, a large sedan came roaring out of a side road, spinning its wheels and spitting gravel, and slid to a stop behind me. Four men spilled out of its flapping doors. One was holding a stick, another dragged a chain. I jumped back in my car and sped off. They followed me for ten miles to the highway, where I was able to lose them in the heavy Sunday traffic. For quite a while after that, I drove a different route on my way to or from the farm.

Our friends were never able to return to their farm.

Dorothea Lange, *Winters, CA,* 1943. Photonegative, 2¼ x 2¼ inches.

The Letter

Kaitlin Deasy

Unlike the student who can explain why cylinder A is passive
While cylinder B is gaseous and reactive,
You can hold Love and Grief up to the light and still
Not know how to extract one from the other.
Omit cause and effect because life is rhetorical.
In one moment, you are seduced like the trees in a sun-choked grove
Up to your throat in warmth and punchy under the spell
Of an untranslatable Exaggeration, which makes the world
Read aloud like a tender erotic, tragicomic letter addressed to you.
What will you write back, in correspondence with this place?
For that is all it is, your being here in feeling and in thought.
Observe the saplings, vertical in their youth, binding together over time
Branches snaking around the waists of their leaned-on neighbors
Much like us, in spite of our best-feigned efforts to remain unattached.
How you choose to live is one way of writing meaning into the margins
Where you answer with love and are changed by grief.

Jenny Long, *Walk,* 2014, ink and watercolor, 22 × 17 inches

Susan Putnam, *Untitled #226*, 2013, charcoal, crayon, gouache, 19 × 24 inches

Commuting in the Valley of Shadows

Susan Starbird

MILE 0 Thinking not of the journey but of my destination, I cautiously creep my car out from under oaks mistdripping in midsummer fog and onto the raggedy country road.

Thursday begins. Neighbors rush-hour downhill while dog-walkers hike up, nosing newspapers as they wander, dogs zigzagging phone poles, aloofly observed by roosting raptor. Cyclist huffing on his morning constitutional. Daily I wave. Daily he scowls, huffs.

I proceed to the intersection. On autopilot; still snoozy. Stop, sip from a cup, contemplate, crack the window to bring in the day. Choice: freeway versus backroad. Thirty mins. versus thirty-five. Freeway a ratatat-race of citybound tradesmen. Back route the open road between golden hills rolling up to summer's silver sky.

Decision: back road.

MILE 1.1 Licheny oaks layer away in the mist, paler and paler as they fade into redwoods on the ridgetops.

Seamlessly, I thread between potholes. Pavement worse than ever now. Intentionally untended rural roads decomposing to gravelly goatpaths, Western civ devolving. Future: dirt roads + broadband.

Radio on — *krrchkle rsssch krrchkle* — radio off. Thrush gurgles amid crowcaw now audible.

MILE 4.2 Rearview mirror. Get your snout out of my exhaust, asshole.

Flash of redwinged blackbird, song trailing. So pass me already, Mr. Mustang. Saw you Tuesday, too. Do we work the same shift?

Road a narrow corridor overhung by willows. Wildlife-watchful, I eyeball side-to-side. Tailgating Mustang whoopdedoos over potholes, while my car senses acorn under tire, princess-pealike. Six inches of clearance, hard suspension, teeth clackety-clacking. There, he passed. Double yellow so what. Asking for it.

MILE 5.9 A remembered feature photo—decades ago: young woman crushed in VW. Slender, smooth hand hanging out the window, fingers limp.

Zeroing in on a dangling hand through history's loupe. Victim would have been my age now.

Old. I'm old. Strike that. *Age ain't nuttin' but a numbah.*

Redtail: *screeeee.*

Bobcat crossed here one time. See bobcats oftener lately. Fog sluices up the canyon, roiling over the eucalyptus windbreak on the far side. Inland heat a colossal fog-suck.

Race through the radio pre-sets:

— *take over control of the no-fly zone, krssssh krrchkle the effort to protect civilians through aggressive airstrikes* —

— *school lunch menu in the krrchkle* —

— *trains delayed by up to an hour and commuters are advised* —

— *Krrchkle* —

Hopeless. Off. Sip.

MILE 7.1 Slowdown for the village. Dory hoisting the flag over the P.O. Phoned our house once to remind me letter I mailed was two cents short. Postmistress sees all, knows all. I'm just passing through, honestly.

Hitched up in front of the store, a remuda of Ford F250s. Dairymen, sheepmen convened round the wateringhole for the morning gab. Trucks manure-splashed and battered, rusted: roan, palomino, sorrel. In a truck's bed two restless collies.

Farmers thinking about commuters: *hope they're just passing through. Are there more like them coming from where those came from?*

Village ends, open road just ahead. Last chance to pull over and let them pass: Camry, BMW, Subaru, Prius. Single-file streaming through the chicane, Le Mans acceleration, riding nose to tailpipe.

Freeway refugees. Sudden brake lights, smoking tires puff, diving Camry sped too soon into the blind curve. There go those turkeys again, crossing. Turkeys in a row, poking along beak to tailfeathers slowing traffic better than any sign. Locals thinking: *What this town needs is more turkeys.*

MILE 7.5 Skittering eucalyptus slash sweeps across road.

— day after NATO agreed to take over command of krssssh —

MILE 8.2 Trundling to hilltop ahead, school bus slows for coldquaking hooded kiddiehuddle. Yellowflashyellow. Skip past before outflips the stop sign.

— economy shrank krrchkle forecast —

MILE 9.3 Shrine on the gravelly roadbank. Oily stain on pavement remains, two years after teenagers torched. Sad scary. Pink-themed memorial constantly grows. Rose-hued portraits, pallid plastic flowers, ragged ribbons, trinkets, messages pile on, pile up, spill out, fluttershred. Seen at 60 mph.

MILE 9.9 Ahead, Camry briefly brakes, noticing piebald pattern in the shadows: covert cop. Cruisers common as ticks. But never around for Mr. Mustang.

MILE 10 Forsale sign flashes: roadhouse, closed years. 'Nother boondock business bites the dust. Some of my best clients went broke. Jinxed?

If your receivables are less than 10 percent uncollectable you're probably being too cautious, my father told me.

Risk management, I utter aloud to self, addressing the road ahead.

Farmstand promising fresh veg. Squash for cash in slot. Mountain lion yonder is only a tawny treestump mirage. Fall for it every day, do a double-take, duh. Still looking for that mountain lion hubby saw near here in bottomlands' dawnfog. Clearly a cat, bound-bounding across the highbeams, long tail lashing the light. Come back, cougar. I wanna be your witness.

MILE 10.9 Vultures flush from yesterday's bloated buck at a known deer crossing. Note to self: avoid this road at night. One night headlights' strobe captured spectral doe inches from speeding fender. Delayed palpitations, driver's wide eyes like deer-in-the-headlights.

MILE 12.3 Grit still sheens pavement where the creek overspilled last winter. Could kayak upstream to here from sea ten, twelve miles across flooded pastures, shocked Holstein heifers bolting. But for trees' tangle in current. Sally drowned in tree. Under fourteen or eight or six inches of turbid water. Daffodils we scattered in her memory, 1992. One woman standing in for womankind. One loss all. Daffodils.

MILE 12.4 Outrage: rural roadside dumpers left a mattress, sofa. Where once was found a body in a sleeping bag stumbled upon by cyclist. Female corpse, of course, of course.

Egret strides away from the passing car on lankystorky legs. A white crownfeather lifts, floats.

— *more troops krrchkle rsssch reconnaissance flights* —

Six, seven yearling horses grazing. Potato farm. Harvestime I'll stop. Return of potato farms, vineyards coming in, these fancy horses. Dairies hanging on.

Remembering daffodils.

Ad hoc dumpsite on the lonesome road. Collected by me one day in roadside cleanup: 1000 matchbooks advertising Mi Ultimo Refugio restaurant. Last stop for stovetop, greasy vent hood, coffee cups, carpeting, crap.

— Mi UL-ti-mo re-FU-gio: *the last refuge of scoundrels is* . . . what? Xenophobia.

MILE 12.6 Caution, cars stop for clutch of kittens crossing from house to milking barn. Glossy chrome milk tanker parked outside in dull morning light.

Caution, dead raccoon crossing. Often come in pairs, where's the oth — ? There.

Radio on:

— beep-beep, 'n' beep-beep, yeah!—

Yeah? No. Imagine there's no Beatles, easy if you try.

— price of gasoline rose krrchkle consecutive day as —

Off.

MILE 17 On the right: white cattle, white horse, white sheep, barbwire fence a white dotted line of whitesheepwoolly Bottsdots. Dotting tan hill: specks of windblown white plastic trash. Charolais something new. Sheep then Herefords then Angus now Charolais. White, brown, black, white. Sheep no match for coyotes. Cattle better. Better yet, throw in a mean llama—ptooey! Fluffy Great Pyrenees fun to find in a flock.

As always, I scan the slopes hopefully. Jackpot: cougar. Or please a coyote. Bobcat: cool. Settle for a weasel. In descending order of charismatic megafauna: after weasel, what? Taxonomy.

Camry cuts off toward the coast; adios, comrade.

Crushing gray sky over dry wideopen wide-open valleyscape sweeps out to ocean. Only companions on this stretch of road now are phone wires looping alongside. Agoraphobic, agoraphonic land. Loneliness or alienation, same diff?

— *I am a lineman for the counteeeeee*

Wires singing old song.

— *still on the liiiiiiine*

Old. Don't think about what's ahead: daffodils, daffodils all the way down.

The future today: Bills due. Call client. Thinking of work, pitapat, feel a little flush of flightfight. Wonder the name of the hormone, cortisomething.

What to say. Composing argument for new strategy, new campaign. How to talk clients out of status quo.

MILE 18.1 'Tis the season of the flattened possum and sailrabbit. *Though I drive through the valley of shadows . . . I will fear no . . .*

Back in '80s Charles said *tomorrow I fly to LA to meet with the client and tell them they should hand out free coffee mugs. So this,* said I, *is how we're gonna get rich?* Charles: *Advertising is not going to solve the problem for this company.* I: *Such a saint should be in seminary.*

Neither of us belonged in the ad biz back then, when money was still on the move, fax was cutting edge, and six flights up I lugged a first-generation portable computer. Young and industrious as so many ants.

Nuttin' but a numbah.

Left the city for reasons forgotten, but would not trade these hills sky sheep oaks rattlesnakes barns road wind ponds cows vultures to author a memoir, autobiography of an ant.

— *and if it snows that stretch down south won't ever stand the strain* —

Am I really listening to this that clings like a jingle in the mind's ear? Offswitch.

What keeps me in the business now is inertia, not stillness, but trotting along the samsaric treadmill until something pushes me off it. Think you're escaping and run into yourself.

MILE 19.3 Cross the commutal divide where cell service crackles to life.

Swarm of chartreuse-shirted cyclists taking the early route out as I head in. It's downhill and smooth sailing ahead; in the rearview looms the groundcloud I've escaped. Sometimes summer fog is so dense, so thick, so bleak and black I believe the massif parked on my horizon is solid.

Give the clients what they want. What harm can it do? Might even do some good. Later sell them what they nee—

Phone buzz. Jesus!

"Ted, that you?"

— *Krrchkle krssssh krrchkle.* Sigh. Shout.

"Can you hear me? No? Yes? What up. Uh-huh."

"Did you see the focus group report? Aye-yi-yiyiyi. Yeah, good news we found out now. Bad news is what it's going to take to fix the offer— "

"Well that's what the pilot's for, to market-test— "

"What to believe, the original research or the focus group? One batch of consumers versus— "

"Anyway, what about the decisions they make after our— "

"Uh-huh. And someone inside the client to protect the brand ID. Logo cop, uh-huh. And the broadcast buy— "

"You do that, and I'll wrap up the budget. A spreadsheet. Soon as I get to the office, yeah. Fifteen, twenty."

"'kay. 'kay. Bye."

MILE 22.1 The whole thing, or just my little slice of the pie: spreadsheets.

Traffic bunches at country school crossing, pokes its way all the way into town behind the feed truck. Lumbering feed trucks, school buses the price for freeway refuseniks. Inching our way into town while caffeine kicks in.

A wake-up long ago. Unforgettable the day a bankruptcy trustee phoned to say we're coming after you as well as your deadbeat client.

Outside looking in, people see only the ads, the two or three ad insertions you ordered, not the sucker-punch that's part of the quotidian schlep.

MILE 22.4 Shuffling jogger in DayGlo orange. Colors jump in the summer-dulled landscape, luring bee's-eye. So cold, so cruel is the world's beauty. In the end, you are there only with your body, home alone within your body, and that's the loneliest place of all, and a shock after lifelong shuffling on a hamster wheel believing that you are not alone.

MILE 23 City limit sign: Pop. 55,178 . . . minimart . . . huddle of day laborers, yearning eyes asking *Is there a job inside that car?* Somebody's hiring, somewhere, maybe Singapore.

There but for grace of god. My work offshoreable. Shoveling manure not. Highest and best use of our Master's degrees, I said to hubby, shoveling into our garden. We can always do this for a living, when everything else is gone.

Masters wanted for stallmucking. For *servicing* clients, some stutter, as in studs or cynical satisficing. Business leaches out morality, leaves you salted and somewhat satisficed. *Your investment in your MBA is completely amortized within five years,* intoned my accountant. Meaning written-down-written-off, or meaning aged-knowledge-croaked I asked. Forgot answer proves point.

Old. Could I do it again?

When to stop, smell the ceanothus.

Hang on awhile longer, working. Contracting way better than employment, boss, timecard. *If you don't come to work Sunday don't bother coming in Monday.*

Gnat bats ineffectually against inside of windshield.

And now the demise of unions. Used to be the only houses with ski boats in the driveway were union families. Dull work, assembly line.

What to do with a motorboat but put gas in it. What MPG a 250hp Evinrude? Rude turns kick big wake: fun. An hour might get it out of my system. Should do it just once: rent one and boof some waves under a summerblue sky. Why/why not. T-shirt slogan: *I'll try anything once, maybe twice.*

Walter Mitty thing, to be unionized. Greener, grassier, over there; sere here. I coulda been an employee, before Before. Two roads converged in a wood, etc., etc.

Today: Update budget. Call client. Whip out work-in-progress. Pay bills. Lunch meeting no big deal. Could have worn jeans instead of this ant-black suit. What appearance is being kept up here anyhow?

Corporations can't oppress if one opts out of consuming. Water from the tap a better option. Gas from the corp, no options there. ChevronShellExxon the last brand standing. iOptOut of consumerism in a day without an Apple. Easy if you try.

And now the unions. And the infinitesimal X percent of the pop. realizing a monstrous Y percent of the income, blah blah Gini coefficient, wages stagnant for decades, and economists say you can kiss your utils goodbye.

And we antworkers trapped by externalities.

Today: priorities. Budget, client call. Lunch. Now thoroughly awake.

— guess I need a small vacaaaaation —

Echoes. Now those damn jinglejangling whining Wichita lineman's-lines are stuck in my head. Wichita, Ouachita, Kansas, Kansa. Places named for people, people transformed by places. To wonder about while traffic piles up behind the crawling feed truck heading into town. My special dream-sites: snowswept blue dome in McMurdo's albedo; sunset-colored canyon of Wadi Rum; gentle honk of the nuthatch in a pine overlooking The Lake.

How this happens, this attachment to a map-speck. One: you read/hear about a place. Or see a photo, movie. Or remember. I imagine a black-and-white snapshot of campers.

Two: form a mental picture of The Lake, complete with the smell of dust and kapok.

Three: pin the place on the map of personal geography.

Four: every time you think of the place, up pops the picture, real or not. Pop! vision of the tree-fringed lake. Pop! smell of pine, baked canvas. Pop! call of the nuthatch. Popup by popup, the placename becomes a towering shrine buttressed by your devotions. All this embodied in two words: *The Lake.* Names evoke —

— Like brands, I say aloud.

The guy in front of me creeps along at 35 in a 45-mile-an-hour zone. *Grrrrr.*

Yes, like brands, w/attributes, expectations, stories attached. These places promise transformation for only the price of passage.
You don't need to go there to have the experience. The fantasy is sufficient.

Recalling the first time I fell in love with a place.

I sat in my diapers on the scabby sisal carpet in the fluttering glow of the blackandwhite television. Commercial invites me to deliver myself into the embrace of the newly opened Magic Kingdom.

Drooling, I cannot take my eyeballs off Mickey, Snow White, the castle, the distant thudding efflorescence of fireworks.

When finally experienced reality of Disneyland, at age nine, raw longing crushed by devastating realization. Yearn too long too ardently, disappointment inevitable.

And here, now, this damn truck backing up traffic.

Too late or not to set out for Mecca?

Hopeful not too late for wow. Question of how.

What the —— ? Far ahead on the left, out of a cypress, looms a UFO: round, and trailing a long tail. What —— ? Kites across the road as the car approaches. Closing in, I see a — what — ?

A peacock. Afloat with its weighty tail drooping like a landing airplane. Brakes in midair, crashes and vanishes into a sea of wind-torn weeds.

Did that really happen just now? Did that peacock really cross the road?

MILE 24.7 Arriving downtown a letdown. Impatiently, fingertappingly, waiting at stoplight staring at Victorian lamppost. Lashed to it a faded ragflapping pink plastic holiday bow at eye level, last remnant of Chamber of Commerce's Christmas cutification. Why dedecorate now, anyway? Christmas in only six months.

Descending hot pressure on the bladder. Fingers tap tap. Fingers drum drum. Green light. One more mile. A plan, to do, first thing: open office, grab bathroom key, dash for it.

MILE 25.5 Journey's end. Park. Grab briefcase, laptop, gym bag, and run toward the gates of hell, pausing momentarily at the threshold to straighten my collar.

Isela Carreras, Grade 12, *Different,* charcoal, 18 × 18 inches

The Origin of a Piano

Sierra Sabec

A bang of the left hand
got the right hand singing

The immense creativity
that differed the white plump key
from the skinny black one awed me so

like a lady planting flowers
row by row by row
in pattern
with exquisite care

And the flowers danced
the right hand sang
and she captured this moment

with a whisk of her hand
and
the piano was born

Lullaby for Seamus

Composition and lyrics by Agnes Wolohan von Burkleo

Ashley Eva Brock, *Shoe Creature,* 2012, handmade leather shoes and painted organza costume. Performance by Asia Wong; digital photograph by Aubrey Trinnaman.

Charles Dickens and Ferguson

Elisabeth Ptak

I'm not going to tell you the story the way it happened. I'm going to tell it the way I remember it. —Charles Dickens, *Great Expectations*

I FIRST read Charles Dickens in snatches of elegant script on the murals in the Pick Quick Room, the cafeteria at the Famous-Barr department store in Jennings, a north St. Louis County suburb that borders the now infamous Ferguson, Missouri.

Famous-Barr was the centerpiece of the Northland shopping center, a mid-century modern complex of brick, exposed rock, and stainless steel that opened in 1955. That was the same year Rosa Parks, taking the bus home from work as a seamstress in a Montgomery, Alabama department store, refused to give up her seat to a white passenger. Northland was the pride of St. Louis—an architectural older sibling of sorts to the sleek and elegant Gateway Arch, the iconic symbol of America's westward expansion that would be built ten years later, downtown, on the banks of the Mississippi River. You may be familiar with Northland. You may have seen it on TV or read about it on Twitter. It's the shopping center that became the staging area for police and militia during the Ferguson protests immediately after the shooting of Michael Brown, an unarmed black teenager, by a white police officer in August 2014.

Famous-Barr at Northland was the first place my mother worked to support me and my three brothers when our father became ill around the time it opened. Later, when I was in high school, the shopping center was the place where I bought the guitar I never learned to play. It was where I got shoes for the prom and had them dyed to match my dress. It had a grocery store and a bowling alley and a movie theatre. Everything about Northland—from the signage to the dramatic light fixtures to the atrium staircases—was emblematic of the bright future envisioned for the nation after World War II. It was the "great expectations" of the St. Louis civic and mercantile worlds.

I like to think it was Dickens's language rather than those murals of paunchy men in tights that led me to *The Pickwick Papers* and the author's other novels. The literary pun in the cafeteria's name was surely lost on me when I was a girl, but I understood that those walls were telling a story, and I wanted to read more. The bookmobile came to our school once a month, bringing with it Miss Havisham, Pip, and Magwitch of *Great Expectations,* as well as the *Flower Fairies*, the *Little House* books, and the Bobbs-Merrill "orange" biographies of Madame Curie and of botanist George Washington Carver, who grew up on the Missouri farm where his parents had been enslaved.

My own father's family moved to St. Louis from their farm in Sedalia, Missouri. (A child had drowned in the well. They lost heart and the farm, too.) They took up residence on a street named Côte Brilliante in a large, four-family flat belonging to my mother's mother. The neighborhood was just a few minutes away from Kensington Avenue, the elegant street memorialized in the movie *Meet Me in St. Louis*.

My parents' story was sort of like the one in the movie, except that the boy-next-door was the boy-in-the-downstairs-flat. Judy Garland, of course, was played by my mother. She was stylish, pretty, and the darling of her family. She drove a shiny new Chevrolet she'd purchased from General Motors, where she worked as a secretary. Not long afterwards, she had an accident and gave up driving for good. It was a setback, but she knew she could always take the bus.

My father was good-looking and showed promise. He certainly was a hard worker. Starting at the age of 16, he labored first as a rodman and chainman on property surveys, then as a pushboat operator on hydrographic surveys for the Army Corps of Engineers. His jobs took him out of town a lot, but after he and my mother were engaged, he filled his spare time away writing declarations of love that were delivered to her by U.S. mail, sometimes twice a day.

Despite its name, Côte Brilliante—French for "shining hill"—would eventually lose its luster. After they married, and after the birth of my two older brothers, my parents moved into a new, two-bedroom, 960-square-foot brick house in working-class Walnut Park, a few miles from Ferguson. By then, my father drove to work downtown, carrying his drafting tools in a velveteen-lined leather case about the size of a book, in which the calipers, the protractors, and every ruler of every shape had a designated place.

As far as I know, there was not yet any indication of the illness that would keep my father hospitalized from the time I was five years old until I was a junior in high school. When he got sick, my mother must have scrambled to find places for us kids so she could go back to work. I was enrolled hastily, mid-year, at the Walnut Park public school kindergarten, where I was graded on, among other things, "Social and Spiritual Growth" (Obeys willingly; Controls feelings; Is kind). The following fall I started first grade under the tutelage of Sister Angeline at St. Louise de Marillac, where I learned to be fervent and to sing *Frère Jacques*.

Our Walnut Park neighbors were German, Polish, Irish, and Italian, with a multilingual mix of customs and nationalities, but they had two things in common. They had all left the Old Country or the

Old Neighborhood, closer to downtown, with dreams of finding a better place to live. And they were all white.

One neighbor operated a beauty parlor in her basement. The Pevely Dairy truck parked every night in front of another house on the street because the milkman lived there. On hot summer evenings, we'd scramble for the ice chips in the back of the iceman's truck with our friends, the iceman's children. The corner bar, a beer garden, was called Shady Grove. Walnut Park in the 1950s was the epitome of post-war working-class America, with both prosperity and Tang on the horizon. And yet, what was that frisson of discontent in the adults' voices? What were they nervous about?

Occasionally, a young black man would walk down the middle of the street on, say, an August afternoon. He'd carry a flat of strawberries balanced on his shoulder. He'd call out "straw-bae-rees" in deep cadenced syllables that brought his customers outside for quick business transactions. But those berries were only a temporary visa into the neighborhood. When they were gone, so was he. The voices continued to conjure fear in front-porch conversations in the summer and in knotty-pine-walled basements in the winter. What were they afraid of?

Eventually, I understood they were afraid of the neighborhood "changing," which was code for Negroes or, as they would have put it, "niggers," moving in. Though I didn't hear this talk from my parents, I heard it from relatives and other adults, seemingly nice people in every way but this one. The grown-up talk sounded wrong to me, and it felt contagious. "In the little world in which children have their existence," wrote Dickens in *Great Expectations,* "whosoever brings them up, there is nothing so finely perceived and so finely felt as injustice."

In fact, racism was and still is as insidious in my home town as the humidity, and just as suffocating. No one needed proof that these unknown black people would be bad for the neighborhood. They took it on faith, or so it would seem since most people at that time were churchgoers. Many neighbors posted "Not for Sale" signs. To emphasize that God was on the side of white people, someone burned a cross on the front lawn of the first black family to buy a house on our street.

And things did change. Walnut Park is now one of the most crime-ridden parts of St. Louis, but the reasons are neither simple nor exclusive to my old neighborhood.

The Interstate Highway Program of 1956 was designed to create a national system of roads. Missouri was one of the first states to take advantage of the funding provided by the government when it authorized work on what would become I-70, a highway that stretches from Maryland to Utah. Locally, I-70 was supposed to lighten traffic on city streets and make commuting to work downtown easier, but instead it facilitated white flight across the county line to close-by suburbs.

And so began another sort of westward expansion—not the Lewis-and-Clark type memorialized by the Gateway Arch but a westward exodus from the city of St. Louis to places like Ferguson, then to suburbs beyond—animated by what we now call racial profiling, and institutionalized by both *de jure* and *de facto* segregation. Businesses moved away. Schools deteriorated. The economy tightened. Joblessness increased, and so did crime. For those left behind in the crumbling inner city, poverty gave way to hopelessness. Nobody wants to live in a dangerous neighborhood.

By 1994, Famous-Barr was shuttered, and in 2005 it was torn down. But for much of my childhood, my mother and I often went there on Saturdays, with lunch in the Pick Quick Room a special treat. On Sundays, though, she took my brothers and me to visit our father at the Missouri State Hospital, founded in 1864 as the St. Louis County Lunatic Asylum. She had never taken up driving again, so we boarded the Goodfellow bus for the first leg of our journey. The name was jolly in a Dickensian kind of way, but the visits seldom were.

The bus meandered through areas where the streets seemed a little dangerous. Why? I suppose I had a notion it was because they had already "changed." But they seemed livelier, too. Through the bus window, I read posters for club dates featuring Bobbie Blue Bland, B. B. King, Ike and Tina Turner. Finally, after we'd made a transfer or two, I'd see the great dome of the hospital come into view. Designed by the architect William Rumbold, it matched his design for the dome of St. Louis's historic Old Courthouse, where in 1846 slave Dred Scott sued, unsuccessfully, to be a free man.

Dred Scott is buried at Calvary Cemetery, and so are my father and mother. Unlike so many St. Louis neighborhoods, Calvary has never been segregated. The vast burial ground established in the mid-19th century is located about halfway between Walnut Park and Ferguson on West Florissant Avenue. It's huge—there are thousands of gravesites—but if you stop at the office near the imposing granite entrance you can get a map to your family plot and a guide to the graves of notable people interred there. They include playwright Tennessee Williams and his sister Rose, who was the inspiration for Laura in *The Glass Menagerie*; designers Charles and Ray Eames; and a Munchkin from the *Wizard of Oz* movie. Dred Scott—free at last—lies in one of the most prominent sections, and hundreds of people visit his grave each year, according to cemetery staff.

Every once in a while, I drop by my old neighborhood—not in real life, but on Google Earth. The camera shows the house that I grew up in is still there, and it still looks pretty much the way I remember it. A sycamore still grows in the back yard. My brothers played ball in that alley. Though I know there are few, if any, whites living in the neighborhood, from the perspective of Google Earth there's no telling the color of the men, women, and children who live there now.

Studies show that most people, including police officers, are more likely to attribute criminal behavior to blacks than whites, as we have seen in Ferguson. But the white people in St. Louis and the mostly white Ferguson police aren't the only ones with a bias. Though it's tempting, I can't call them to task unless I examine my own conscience. In fact, I catch myself doing racial profiling all the time—when I "notice" a black person walking down a street. Or bicycling! A black person in Lycra? When I avoid certain neighborhoods or at the very least lock my car doors, hunch down, drive faster. When I wonder if I would have joined the protests in Ferguson and am secretly grateful I'm thousands of miles away in California. When I notice what's different about another person rather than what we have in common, with skin color the most obvious of those differences. None of my best friends are black.

Pip, the boy of the great expectations in Dickens's novel, describes a fateful day when, thanks to an anonymous benefactor, his life took a new and unexpected course. "That was a memorable day to me for it made great changes in me. But, it is the same with any life. Imagine one selected day struck out of it, and think how different its course would have been."

I imagine August 9, 2014.

Then, "Pause you who read this," says Pip, "and think for a moment of the long chain of iron or gold, of thorns or flowers, that would never have bound you, but for the formation of the first link on one memorable day."

I pause and think.

The tanks and other military vehicles brought in during the early protests in Ferguson are gone for now. Small businesses have recuperated, or not, from damage done or from the decrease in trade since then. Teenage girls are once again buying dresses at Northland, though at Target instead of Famous-Barr, yet I see I am bound to them, not so much by our shared shopping habits as by the accident of birth, by geography, and by history. And the boys? I am bound now to them, too.

Ido Yoshimoto, *Untitled,* from the series *Astral Planes,* 2014, indigo on cypress, 30 × 24 inches

As Light Escapes

Elizabeth Herron

Bent to the house of leaves and string
I forage for peas in the garden,

split the chrysalis cradles
with a thumb—green pearls

in my palm. I eat them raw—sun
on my back, then go in

and fold into the wicker chair.
On the wall the Chinese painting—

bare branches, blue-gray sky,
Vs of white birds lifting up.

Like that, I think, we will leave
our dark husks

as light escapes a closed room
when you open the door.

Micheleen Tolson, *Cyanotype Leaf,* 2014,
ink and bleach, 17 × 11 inches

roper Cup consists of 4 small teeth, seated on the top of the Seed Bud
posed flower is composed of numerous Pipe shaped flowers in the Disk, (the
Disk being lengthened out into a long head) and 8 or 10 Tongue shaped flowers
the Rays.
flowers in the Disk are cylindrical, short, & their mouth is cut into five
sharp pointed teeth. The little flowers in the Rays are Tongue shaped, 3 times
long as the common Cup & sharp pointed
ies of the flowers in the Disk are 5 fine hairs, inserted into the Pipe of the flower
Their tips are longer than the Chives, & are united together, forming a hollow
cylinder. The flowers in the Rays have no Chives.
stil of the flowers in the Disk. the Seed Bud is under the seat of the proper
wer & is oblong & 3 cornered, they are separated from each other by a Chaff
ke hollow Leaf, of the length of the Seed Bud, & one of them surrounding each
stil of the flowers in the Rays, the Seed Bud is similar to those in the Disk,
They have no Style nor Tip.
er of the Seeds none
d of the flowers in the Disk is single one following each little flower,
ey are long, 4 cornered & little bent, & crowned with 4 small teeth, being
proper Cup, Seed of the flowers in the Rays are similar to these.
t of the Seed is of a long conic figure, twice the length of the common Cup
Chaff is the length of the Seed, and is in the form of one half of a hollow
linder, when split into two surrounding one half of every Seed, & separa-
ng them from each other.
talk is ridged & is branched out alternately.
ves have short Leaf Stalks and are placed alternately, the lower Leaves are
vided almost to the foot stalk into 3, each part is of an ovally sharp
inted figure, the middle part is largest, the edges are cut like very large Saw
eeth each of the 3 parts of the Leaf has a straight fiber along the middle,
ith a few circular ones on each side of it extending upwards. The Leaves
bout the middle of the Plant, are not so deeply divided as the lower ones
nd the Leaves at the top are intire, only the edges of all are cut like
aw teeth. Towards to top of the Plant, the Leaf Stalks grow gradually
horter. The Leaves are all harsh to the touch and the lower ones
most so
he Plant grows in moist ground & is about 3 or 4 feet high, the
... are yellow & stand single on the tops of the branches.
Flower in Augu

Help Me Out, Billy

Jan Dederick

Billy, I know I have no business taking issue
with "the most popular living American poet," but you
hit a nerve when you said you have "no interest in being

confronted with anyone's trauma." I'm not here to interest you
in mine, for sure, but to invite you to reflect a while:
it seems to me, a novice, Billy, that your poems simply arise

like New Jersey August sweat, shoot like New Hampshire August stars.
Many poems, though, curl nascent in history's *piñatas,*
needing life's cudgel to blow them free. All over the floor, poems: messy.

But, no trauma, you say: you only want a poem to
"linguistically pleasure" you. Yet, in a dream, Poetry told me
something else: that she is a bridge to the heart.

So I'm confused, Billy. Help me out here.
You said, "83 percent of poetry is not worth reading."
Those odds are worse than passing the California Bar Exam.

And Billy, you said you "get frustrated" teaching students
who lack "what it takes," who'd "do better to study laying tile
than poetry." Reflecting on your words, while brushing my hair,

I look deeply into the mirror to see if I am
a person who would frustrate you in class, or who'd pleasure you
linguistically. A sense of rhythm you said, *sine qua non:*

there's a turbine in my hips that lifts me,
a metronome in my bone, driving, driving.
Would their bebop pass your poet's muster?

And metaphor, the other must-have, that connection between
pedestrian and lunatic: the hair brush, for example,
and a golf club. I can drive an image onto the green, under par,

putt a pun out of Villanelle's bunker, poetic birdie.
And even alliterate a little bit.
Does that make me a worthy candidate to play

in the Fields of the Word with you?
Could I aspire to join the 17 percent?
And even if not, surely teacher and student agree:

83 percent of poetry may not be worth reading,
but all of it's worth writing.
So help me out, Billy. I'm still sitting here, brush in hand.

Sawyer Rose, (opposite) *Metamorphosis,* 2014, silver solder, oil on panel, 28 × 28 inches; (above), *Costanoa Coral,* 2014, silver solder, oil on panel, 14 × 11 inches

AWESOME

Madeleine S. Butcher

Awesome has taken on a daily feel
as in—"I'll have fries with that."

Our waiter writes it down, nodding.
"Awesome," he says looking up,
"Anything else?"

That awe...

as in feeling so small
before a thing so vastly greater than we,
a thing embodying a profound truth
which we can sense but not ever truly know,

...should be applied to an order of fries...
is a thing in itself of great wonder and incredulity,
which often but not always,
stands side by side with
incomprehensible idiocy
laced with such sweetness
that one feels oddly and deliriously hopeful.

Mark Ropers, *Kite at Stinson Beach,* 2014, watercolor, 10 × 11 inches

Writers and Artists

LESLIE ALLEN is a Sausalito artist and architect whose favorite environment and ecology are West Marin. Imaginary ancestors include New England transcendentalists and Laura Ingalls Wilder.

HEATHER ALTFELD teaches at California State University, Chico and is a member of the Squaw Valley Community of Writers. Her recent publications include poetry in *Narrative Magazine, Cimarron Review, Pleiades, ZYZZYVA, Poetry Northwest.*

A self-taught artist living in Oakland, MARSHA BALIAN's attraction to Point Reyes leads her there almost every week to hike.

EVA BELL is twelve years old and enjoys spending time with her animals and cartooning.

LUCAS BENJAMIN is a poet/musician and woodworker living in the Shasta bioregion of California.

ASHLEY EVA BROCK is a fashion and costume designer, creature maker, and textile artist living in Bolinas. Her work explores healing, magic, playfulness, and abstraction while focusing on ecological sustainability.

MADELEINE SWIFT BUTCHER writes poetry, fiction, and true-life stories with recipes. She teaches ballet and Pilates and is a member of Westside Women Writers.

ISELA CARRERAS is a senior at Tomales High School in Advanced Placement Art. She enjoys drawing in charcoal and is inspired by Japanese art. In the fall she'll be studying criminal justice at San Francisco State University.

Fourth grader NATALIE CHAVARRIA likes soccer and basketball and loves riding bikes. Her best friends are Viviana, Ailyn, Natalia, and Izabella.

MICHELLE CHAYES was born in Germany, raised in England, and lived for many years in Inverness with husband Bill and daughters Imogene and Frida. She currently lives in Chileno Valley near Petaluma, California.

PETER CONNORS earned an MS in Physics and a PhD in Molecular Biophysics at the University of Wisconsin-Madison. His research work at UC Bodega Marine Laboratory has included the ecology of shorebirds in California and arctic Alaska, and ecology and conservation of coastal grasslands.

BETTY DAVIDSON is a sixth-grade student at White Hill Middle School in Fairfax, California. She loves to write, act, and have a good laugh.

KAITLIN DEASY grew up in Northern California and attended the University of California at Berkeley, where she earned a Bachelor of Arts in English Literature. She resides north of San Francisco and works as a freelance writer and massage therapist.

JAN DEDERICK of El Cerrito, California is an alternative healthcare practitioner, musician, and poet; 2013 grand prize winner at the Dancing Poetry Festival; co-host of Poetry Express, Berkeley; co-editor of *Poetalk,* journal of Bay Area Poets' Coalition.

TOBI EARNHEART-GOLD grew up in Bolinas. He is currently studying poetry back east.

TED ECHEVERRIA is a New England native, graduate of Deerfield Academy and Brown University. He moved to West Marin after suffering a stroke in 2008, and has been a participant in programs at the Brain Injury Network of the Bay Area since 2013.

CHARLES ECKART is a painter and etcher who focused on the figure for many years. He changed to landscape after moving to Point Reyes Station, and his work has gradually become more abstract.

JODY FARRELL has been writing since she was nine and is still writing at ninety, drawing on a long-life experience with people, birth, death, small daily wonders, and the extraordinary surround of nature.

ANNE FAUGHT is a West Marin artist, gardener, and long-distance walker. She has returned to her studio after years of teaching, delighted to be working and living in paradise.

Born in Texas, poet and nonfiction writer CATLYN FENDLER has lived in Iowa and now roams the rural and the wilds between her home in Larkspur, California and New York City.

For BARBARA R. FINKELSTEIN, home is a triangulation of her native Pennsylvania hills, northern California fogs, and small town Safety Harbor, Florida, full with family, friends, and fellow writers.

VIVIANA VILLALOBOS GONZALEZ is in fourth grade. She loves art and plans on going to college. There are many choices, and she says, "I do not know what the future might bring me."

IZABELLA GUITERREZ is in fourth grade at West Marin School. She loves art, traveling, reading, and riding bikes.

ELIZABETH CAROTHERS HERRON's work appears in *Parabola, Orion, Reflections* (Yale Divinity School), and *Canary: A Literary Journal of the Environmental Crisis.* She has twice been nominated for the Pushcart Prize in Poetry.

CHARLES HOEHN was project manager for the construction of the San Francisco-Oakland Bay Bridge in the 1930s. His photo is made available to us by previous contributor Vivian Olds, and the Paul Sevcsik family.

SABINE HOSKINSON is a young writer with a passion for words, aesthetics, and the outdoors. She is working on a collection of personal essays and a short memoir.

ROBERT KRONINGER, a native-born northern Californian, as were both his parents, is a retired judge living in Inverness. His story is excerpted from his unpublished autobiography, *My Life, Chance and Design.*

BOB KUBIK lives at the southern edge of Inverness Park. He paints and draws and makes things as the spirit moves him.

JENNIFER KULBECK is a writer, printer, and outfielder living in San Francisco. She collects stories, pastimes, and household objects from estate sales and is an MFA student at San Francisco State University.

JON LANGDON, California native, still learning, still growing, headed toward the great expanse, but not just yet.

FRANCES LEFKOWITZ is the author of the award-winning memoir *To Have Not,* and a freelance writer, editor, and writing coach. She blogs about writing, publishing, and footwear at PaperInMyShoe.

JUDY LEVIT's mixed media paintings explore inner worlds and reflect her reverence for nature. Her work as a psychotherapist informs and enhances her investigations of internal landscapes and conversations.

JENNY LONG spent her early childhood in San Francisco and Marin. Her studio and home are in the Sierra Nevada foothill communities of Nevada City and Grass Valley.

JACQUELINE MALLEGNI creates minimalist sculpture inspired by Asian aesthetics and philosophy. Ethereal in nature, her artwork reflects the fragility and strength of life and the human spirit.

PAOLA MARTIN is in sixth grade at West Marin School. Since preschool, she has loved art and spends time sketching.

ROY MASH is a long-time board member of Marin Poetry Center. His first full-length book, *Buyer's Remorse,* debuted in 2014.

Now a freshman at Tomales High School, JOCELYN MATA has been writing poetry since fourth grade. She plans to go to college and sees many possibilities ahead.

G. DAVID MILLER teaches at the University of California at Davis, where he has a freshly captured audience every semester for his stories.

T. C. MOORE is an environmental artist from Canada who resides in Petaluma. Her work questions the definitions and boundaries of drawing, painting, sculpture, and fiber arts.

SCOTT MOSSMAN studied creative writing at King Hall, University of California at Davis, and now practices immigration law. He lives in Oakland with his wife, Somjintana, and their two sons.

TERRY MURPHY is a builder and painter. His heroes include Wyeth, DeKooning, Diebenkorn, and Lincecum. He is currently working on a series of paintings on labor and the landscape, and on the mechanics of baseball. He lives in Petaluma, California.

JED MYERS lives in Seattle. *Watching the Perseids* (SPC Press) and *The Nameless* (Finishing Line Press) are 2014 releases. Poems have appeared in *Prairie Schooner, Nimrod, I-70 Review,* and elsewhere.

HAL OBER is a writer and editor in Arlington, Massachusetts. He writes content for educational developers in Massachusetts and California. His blog, *Old Hatch's Almanac,* recently turned five.

DENISE PARSONS is author of the novel *After the Sour Lemon Moon* (2014). Her work has appeared in the magazines *Kindred* and *Taproot.* She lives and works in San Francisco.

An Israeli-born concert pianist residing in New York city, ADAH PINCHUK HYMAN began painting in her sixties. She cherishes her visits with family in Point Reyes, where the natural beauty is a source of deep inspiration.

ELISABETH PTAK is a writer, editor, and collagist who lives in Inverness.

SUSAN PUTMAN, once a practicing research biochemist, gave up science to practice art. Her artwork includes photo silkscreen, charcoal drawing, and mixed media. She lives in San Rafael, California.

CHRIS REDING is a painter and writer. This quote from Theodore Roethke hangs on her refrigerator: "Art is the means we have of undoing the damage of haste. It's what everything else isn't."

ERIN RODONI's poems have been published in *Best New Poets 2014, Colorado Review,* and *Verse Daily,* among others. She holds an MFA from San Diego State University.

MARK ROPERS is a watercolorist and member of Point Reyes Open Studios. He is interested in presenting thoughtful, mood-evoking paintings of landscapes, water-related pleasures, and objects of interest.

SAWYER ROSE is a mixed-media and sculpture artist in the San Francisco Bay Area. Using a soldering iron as a paintbrush, she sculpts abstracted organic and botanical forms in layers of molten silver solder.

LARRY RUTH knew Point Reyes before it became a National Seashore. He works in environmental and natural resources policy, and thrives in the remnants of the wild.

SIERRA SABEC is in seventh grade at Lagunitas Middle School. She enjoys writing, playing music, and hanging out with friends and family. She hopes to pursue a career in medicine.

EYTAN SCHILLINGER-HYMAN, 16, attends Lick Wilmerding High School in San Francisco. Eytan enjoys playing bass and sailing on Tomales Bay. His connection to visual art reflects the influences of his grandmother Adah and great grandfather Aaron.

ELIZABETH SHER, Professor Emeritus at California College of the Arts, creates art, film, and artist books in the Bay Area, combining digital technologies with hand work.

MARY K. SHISLER has worked with alternative photography for more than 20 years. A Wisconsin native, she holds an MFA from the University of Wisconsin-Madison.

MARY SIEDMAN has lived on the Bolinas mesa for more than thirty years. As a painter, she concentrates on exposing the light and movement of her natural surroundings.

SUSAN STARBIRD is a Sonoma County commuter, dreamer, and essayist. She has been surreptitiously capturing her mind's wanderings on paper for 50 years. "Commuting" is part of an essay collection on the emotional life of work.

MICHAEL TAYLOR lives on the Inverness Ridge, but spent a career working deep in the belly of the Hollywood beast. He much prefers breathing the crisp, clean air of West Marin.

GARY THORP writes essays, reviews, and other non-fiction, but says, "The shortest distance between two points is often a poem."

MICHELEEN TOLSON founded the New York Textile Design Center in Manhattan, developing artwork for such clients as Calvin Klein, Ralph Lauren, LL Bean, Orvis, and Pendleton. She collects plant specimens for collage while homeschooling her two boys in Sonoma County.

AGNES VON BURKLEO is currently on loan to Ashland, Oregon, where she is putting together a book of her lullabies. She will no doubt be in Inverness again before long.

WARD WALKUP III was born in Palo Alto, California in 1947. He has lived in Cape Town, South Africa and now resides in Hilo, Hawaii.

VANESSA WARING lives and works in Bolinas. Her art is inspired by this coastal landscape, the small community she lives in, and the coyotes she hears at night.

Educated in art and education at Illinois State University, LINDA WEYL has lived in Fair Oaks, California since 2000. She has spent most of her time working in schools or creating something beautiful.

THOMAS WOOD has painted the West Marin landscape for forty-five years. He is a founding member of the annual MALT exhibit, and his studio/gallery is on Nicasio's town square.

IDO YOSHIMOTO, native of Inverness, balances work as artist, arborist, and woodworker. Inspired by excursions along the coast and through the forest, he explores form and textures in wood.

CALIFORNIA'S OLDEST SHELLFISH FARM

SPECIALIZING IN FARMED FRESH OYSTERS FROM THE COOL CLEAN WATERS OF TOMALES BAY

OPEN 7 DAYS A WEEK
BAY SHORE PICNIC AREA

(415) 663-1243

WWW.TOMALESBAYOYSTERCOMPANY.COM

Your creativity is our business!

Joyce Kouffman
musician/composer/teacher
Joyce@JoyceJazz.com
415/663-9176

BEAR VALLEY INN
BED & BREAKFAST

- Located 35 miles north of San Francisco
- One hour from wine country at the gateway to Point Reyes National Seashore
- Surrounded by miles of hiking, bicycling and horseback riding trails.
- A Certified Green Business, organic continental breakfast served daily
- Arrive via bicycle receive a 15% discount or transit and receive a 10% discount!

Booking information & room descriptions
www.bearvinn.com | 415-663-1777

ART GALLERY
WEDDINGS
CONCERTS
& MORE

– Gifts –
– Organic Espresso Bar –
– Organic Produce –
– Yoga Studio –

11250 Highway One
in the heart of Pt. Reyes Station
415-663-1223

ZUMA

SELECT CRAFTS
❖
ETHNIC ARTS

Open Daily
Downtown Pt. Reyes Station
663-1748

Melanie Stone

THE PINE CONE DINER

A Charming, Classic American Diner
"REALLY GREAT FOOD"
Breakfast Served All Day

Espresso, Milkshakes, Beer, Wine,
Local Oysters, House-Made Cobblers,
Gluten-free bread & Gluten-free pancakes

We use Sustainable, Organic, Local
Ingredients Whenever Possible.

Parties & Special Events.

Open 7 Days
from 8 am - 2:30pm

60 4th Street,
1/2 block south of Gas Station
Point Reyes Station
415-663-1536

Flower Power

HOME and GARDEN
P.O. Box 1478 11275 State Route One Point Reyes Station, CA 94956
Tel: 415 663-8221 Fax: 415 663-8839 E-mail: flowerpowermarin@mac.com

EPICENTER
Dana Davidson
COLLECTION

"Dressing West Marin
for over 25 years!"

11100 Hwy 1, Point Reyes Station

www.epicenterpointreyes.com

(415) 663-1239

DANCING COYOTE BEACH
GUEST COTTAGES
Private waterfront cottages overlooking Tomales Bay.
The perfect place from which to do everything,
or to do nothing at all.
FOR INFORMATION & RESERVATIONS
DANCINGCOYOTEBEACH.COM
(415) 669-7200

VITA Collage
A *distinctive* store
11101 State Rte One
Point Reyes Station
415-663-1160

CLAUDIA CHAPLINE GALLERY
Showing Northern California Contemporary Art Since 1987
3445 Shoreline Highway
Mailing: P.O. Box 1117
Stinson Beach, CA 94970
415.868.2308
INFO@CCHAPLINE.COM
WWW.CCHAPLINE.COM

THE STATION HOUSE CAFE
fresh, local & sustainable since 1974
Open 6 days a week
Closed Wednesdays
Main Street • Point Reyes Station
415 663 1515
full bar
garden dining
live music sundays
private dining room for parties and retreats
www.stationhousecafe.com

west marin review

Volume 6

Many thanks to our generous donors!

Lucid Art Foundation
Barry Traub
David and Susan Miller and
the Center for Community
Economic Development

IN-KIND DONORS

Cline Cellars
Tin Barn Vineyards
Toby's Feed Barn
Palace Market

About the *West Marin Review*

West Marin Review
Volume 6, 2015

ISBN 978-0-9822829-4-6

The *West Marin Review* is a publishing collaboration among Point Reyes Books and Steering Committee members Myn Adess, Mark Caballero, Madeleine Corson, Steve Costa, and Doris Ober.

Special thanks to the following local teachers:
Madeline Hope
Rachel Somerville
Colleen Conely
Martha Johnson
Vickisa

SUBMISSIONS FOR VOLUME VII
Submission guidelines: www.westmarinreview.org or info@westmarinreview.org

SUPPORT THE *WEST MARIN REVIEW*
The *West Marin Review* is created through the volunteer efforts of friends, neighbors, artists, and writers. Donations are appreciated (and tax deductible) and volunteers are welcome. To learn how you can help, and to make a donation, go to westmarinreview.org.

West Marin Review
Post Office Box 1302
Point Reyes Station, California 94956
www.westmarinreview.org

FRONT COVER Marsha Balian, *Jill*, 2014, mixed media, 10 × 10 inches

BACK COVER Charles Eckart, *On the Mesa—Point Reyes*, 1992, etching, 3¼ × 5¼ inches